CEREMONIAL
AND
COMMEMORATIVE
CHAIRS
IN GREAT BRITAIN

CEREMONIAL AND COMMEMORATIVE CHAIRS

IN GREAT BRITAIN

CLARE GRAHAM

VICTORIA & ALBERT MUSEUM

Published by the Victoria & Albert Museum 1994, © Trustees of the Victoria & Albert Museum.

ISBN 1 85177 136 0

Produced by Alan Sutton Publishing Ltd., Stroud, Glos.
Printed in Great Britain by The Bath Press, Avon.

Front cover. Joseph Michael Gandy after Sir John Soane. Detail of a design for a new Masonic Hall in Great Queen Street, 1828. Pen and ink with water colour. 2821
Back cover. The Master's Chair of the Old Union Lodge, London. Carved and gilded wood, with crimson leather upholstery, made by John Connop in 1814. W. 70–1982
The President's Chair of the British Medical Association, presented by the Australian branches in 1925. Black bean wood with red leather upholstery, designed by Sir Edwin Lutyens (1869–1944). W. 42–1987

CONTENTS

'A chair must serve to conjure up instantaneously the proud, ornamental, intimidating and quantified spectre of an epoch: the supreme spectre of style. A chair must also serve the most lofty excelsitudes and the most ignominious degradations . . . A chair can even be used to sit on, but with just one condition: that we sit uncomfortably'

Salvador Dali

ACKNOWLEDGEMENTS

The Victoria and Albert Museum is probably the world's greatest repository of the decorative arts, and I was fortunate indeed to be able to draw on its rich collections for this study. The advice and help I received from my former colleagues there was even more important. The place of honour goes to the Furniture and Woodwork Collection, where I first embarked on the project with the encouragement of Simon Jervis. Virtually all its members, past and present, made some contribution, but I must single out Sarah Medlam and Christopher Wilk, who were both kind enough to read the manuscript and make many helpful suggestions. Then I would like to mention Michael Snodin, Susan Lambert and the members of the Sculpture Collection who in succession not only put up patiently with my preoccupation with ceremonial chairs, but even encouraged it. I may add that in its turn the wider experience I gained working on the European Ornament Gallery and the Twentieth Century Gallery, in particular, provided fresh insights for this study. Gwyn Miles and Charles Saumarez Smith generously gave me the opportunity to write up the text in the Research Department, and Jennifer Blain and Lesley Burton have steered it through the publication process. Other V&A colleagues to whom I am grateful for help or advice include Jeremy Aynsley, Marian Campbell, Eoin Shalloo, Isobel Sinden, Meg Sweet, Moira Thunder, Clive Wainwright, Eva White and Linda Woolley.

Outside the museum, I am especially grateful to the Worshipful Company of Carpenters, the Worshipful Company of Fishmongers and the Worshipful Company of Mercers, whose generous financial assistance has made it possible for this study to appear in print. Many other institutions and individuals have been generous about providing access to particular chairs, information, and photographs. In alphabetical order, they are: John Andrews, ARIBA; Katarzyna Kopem Banasik, Keeper of Applied Arts, Princess Czartoryski Foundation, Cracow; Susan Bennett, Library Administrator, Royal Society of Arts; Peter Boughton, Grosvenor Museum, Chester; Philip Crouch, Museums Officer, Wycombe Local History and Chair Museum; P.J.C. Crouch, Clerk, the Worshipful Company of Broderers; Ken Crowe, Keeper of Human History, Southend-on-Sea Museums Service; Peter Day, Keeper of Collections at Chatsworth; The Assistant Clerk of the Drapers Company; The Clerk of the Dyers Company; Carole Edwards, Library and Records Department, Foreign Office; Sheila Edwards, Librarian, Royal Society; Adela Goodall, Assistant Curator (Art), Salisbury and South Wiltshire Museum; Mr St John Gore, Society of Dilettanti; Dr A.B. Grimstone, Pembroke College, Cambridge; John Hamill and Jan Macdonald, Library and Museum of the United Grand Lodge of England; John Hardacre, Curator, Winchester Cathedral; The Revd B.A. Hopkinson, Rector of St Mary's, Whitby; Adrian James, Assistant Librarian, Society of Antiquaries of London; Sally Jeffery, Department of Building and Services, Corporation of London; David Mead, Bursar of Coventry Cathedral; Dr George Minkenberg, Domkapital, Aachen; Enid Nixon, Assistant Librarian, Westminster Abbey; Lord Norton; The Worshipful Company of Parish Clerks; John Phillips, Curator of Maps and Prints, Greater London Record Office and Library; Alan Powers; Brigadier G. Read, Clerk of the Worshipful Company of Vintners; The Revd Nicholas Richards, Rector of St Mary's, Rotherhithe; Colin Richardson, Keeper of Human History, Tullie House Museum, Carlisle; Caroline Roberts, National Maritime Museum; Hugh Roberts, Deputy Surveyor of the Queen's Works of Art and his secretary Henrietta Edwards; Mr G.A. Robertson, Master of Hospital Trinity Hall, Aberdeen; Christopher Starns, Mark Masons' Hall; Colin Stock; Christine H. Stokes, Temple Newsam; David A. Tate, Clerk of the Worshipful Company of Joiners and Ceilers; Tony Taylor, Secretary of Shakespear Lodge; Beth Thomas and Arwyn Lloyd Hughes, Welsh Folk Museum; Steven Tomlinson, Department of Western Manuscripts, Bodleian Library, Oxford; Jan Wallace, National Portrait Gallery; Robin Harcourt Williams, Librarian and Archivist, Hatfield House; Jo Wisdom, Librarian, St Paul's Cathedral; Paul Wood, Honorary Keeper of Otley Museum.

Illustrations

Permission to reproduce illustrations was kindly given by those listed below. All other illustrations are reproduced by permission of the Board of Trustees of the Victoria and Albert Museum.

Fig.6, Tullie House Museum, Carlisle; 9, 121, 131, Wycombe Local History and Chair Museum (9: Guildhall Heritage Exhibition, 131: High Wycombe Central Library); 11, The Royal Society; 35, The Dean and Chapter of St Paul's (photographer: Malcolm Crowther); 36, John Andrews, ARIBA; 41, All Saints' Church, Margaret Street, London; 44, 118, author's photographs; 45, Domkapital, Aachen (photographer: Ann Münchow); 47, The Dean and Chapter of Westminster; 56, The Dean and Chapter of Winchester (photographer: John Crook); 57, 58, National

CHAPTER I
THE SEAT AS A SYMBOL OF AUTHORITY

The origins of the throne

The king made a great throne of ivory, and overlaid it with pure gold.

And there were six steps to the throne, with a footstool of gold, which were fastened to the throne, and five stays on each side of the sitting place, and two lions standing by the stays:

And twelve lions stood there on the one side and on the other upon the six steps. There was not the like made in any kingdom.'

(King Solomon's throne: Chronicles II, ch.10, v.17–19)

The idea that a seat may be used to symbolise the authority of its occupant is very ancient, yet still familiar today. We refer to it whenever we speak of the chair of a professor, or the chairman of a meeting (now usually, and even more graphically, abbreviated to the chair). Actual chairs of state or thrones may be used at many different kinds of assemblies, ranging from coronations and courts of justice to convivial gatherings (figs.1,2,3). Purpose-made beds, stools, and chairs first appeared at a relatively late date, probably in Mesopotamia in the late fourth millennium BC. The introduction of furniture was apparently prompted as much by considerations of status as of increased comfort, and the concept of the

1. *The Coronation of Her Gracious Majesty Queen Victoria*, 1838. Engraving by Henry Thomas Ryall, after Sir George Hayter. 25847A

ceremonial chair seems to be as old as the chair itself. By the time King Solomon ruled in the mid-tenth century BC, the seat already had a long history as a symbol of authority. The description of Solomon's throne given above may stress its uniqueness, but the ancient civilisations of Western Asia and the Mediterranean provide earlier or contemporary parallels for many of its features. Amongst these are its elevated position at the top of a set of steps, its precious materials, the symbolic royal lions and the use of a footstool or footboard.[1] It may well have resembled surviving examples of ancient Egyptian furniture. A further description states its top was 'round behind',[2] which suggests the rolled-over back found on some Egyptian chairs.

It is also possible to move forward in time and find many of the same features reappearing again and again in the thrones of the modern world. There are good practical reasons for this, because the idea of asserting one's authority by sitting comfortably and keeping other, lesser, mortals standing has certain inherent problems. Firstly, it is much easier to dominate people while looking down on them. Unless the seat and its occupant are raised up, they will also vanish from view in any large assembly. It is impractical, not to say unkind, to keep other people standing indefinitely. If they are allowed to sit down as well the ruler's position will still need to be distinguished in some way. A seat used to symbolise its occupant's authority therefore needs to be large, high and visually important.

2. *The Lord Mayor, Aldermen and Common Council of the City of London Corporation in the Council Chamber at Guildhall.* Aquatint by Thomas Sutherland after Richard Dighton, 1825. E611–1903

[1] *See Baker, and* The Furniture of Western Asia, *passim.* [*Frequently-used sources are referred to by a brief title in these footnotes, for the sake of convenience. They are given in full in the bibliography.*]

[2] *I Kings 11, v. 19.*

3. *The Court of Equity or Convivial City Meeting*, mezzotint by Robert Laurie after Robert Dighton, published by J. Smith of Cheapside, 1778. The members of this drinking club include the artist (top right) and the publisher of the print (left, in the Windsor chair), as well as a printer, a silver spoon maker, a sausage maker, an attorney, a bricklayer, a broker, and an auctioneer. They are meeting in the upper room of a London tavern, probably the Bell Savage in Ludgate Hill or the Globe in Fleet Street. E.540–1976

It is not surprising to find that precious and exotic materials have consistently been used in the manufacture of thrones. There is an immediate and obvious connection with the wealth and power of the occupant. This power can also be suggested symbolically through the use of appropriate ornament: the depiction of slaves or vanquished enemies, for instance. A ceremonial chair found in Tutankhamun's tomb is accompanied by a footstool decorated with the nine traditional enemies of Egypt. Representations of their bound figures are placed just where the king's feet would have rested.[3] The point has been more frequently and perhaps more subtly made by supporting thrones and footstools on the legs, or indeed the whole bodies, of powerful animals such as lions and bulls as well as fabulous monsters such as sphinxes and griffins. This suggests kinship as well as mastery: the occupant of such a throne is not simply stronger than these creatures, but also shares their attributes. Hence the special popularity of the lion, king of the beasts, in the decoration of thrones.

Another important reason for conservatism is that concepts of authority are bound up with historical precedent. Rulers have always sought to reinforce their position by calling on tradition, and a break in continuity may only make this more critical. These feelings have helped to preserve old thrones and chairs of state (fig.4). Seats like the Throne of Dagobert in Paris, the Throne of Charlemagne in Aachen and the Coronation Chair in Westminster Abbey gradually accumulated their

[3] *Hollis, p. 83.*

4. 'Seats of the Mighty'. Drawings of ancient thrones by W.B. Robinson, from an article in the *Illustrated London News*, 9 April 1921

own numinous authority through repeated use, as chapter III will show. Respect for tradition also affects the design of new thrones. It will become clear that the biblical descriptions of King Solomon's throne inspired the original decoration of the Coronation Chair. In its turn, the Coronation Chair was the source for some of the nineteenth-century designs discussed in chapter IV.

The description of Solomon's throne does not specify the form of the seat itself. The x-framed chair or stool has been one particularly influential model for the seat of authority. A recent study has traced its history back as far as the mid-third millennium BC, and as far afield as China and Japan. Its use as a symbol of authority in the medieval and modern world derives most directly from the folding stool or *sella curulis* of the Roman magistrate and military commander (fig.5).[4] The x-frame is examined in more detail later on, but its success should not blind us to the many other forms which have also been used for seats of authority. The range of furniture available

[4] *Wanscher.*

5. Rufinus Gennadius Probus Orestes, Consul at Rome in AD 530, seated on a *sella curulis* decorated with lion's heads. This is a stylised image based on a Byzantine model rather than a realistic portrait: ivory diptychs of this kind were commonly presented as personal gifts by consuls to mark their entry to office. The backs of the two panels would be filled with wax and used as writing tablets. 139–1866

in Roman Britain, for instance, was evidently not as wide or as magnificent as it would have been in Italy.[5] Yet apart from the remains of iron folding stools (some decorated with bronze) excavated in this country, there is ample archaeological evidence that other kinds of seats also symbolised authority. Sculptured depictions of divinities, for instance, show them sitting on couches (both straight-backed and semi-circular) and in a type of chair with a solid base and a rounded back sweeping round to form curving sides. This was often woven in basketwork (fig.6), but could also be made from wood and was sometimes sheathed in bronze or even upholstered.[6] It will become apparent that in the Middle Ages an even wider variety of stools, benches, chairs, couches and fixed seats were available for ceremonial use.

It is important to remember from the outset that the rules governing the use of these seats were created by societies which thought in terms of rank, rather than class. Because so little medieval furniture has survived, for instance, it is all too easy to assume that only the wealthy or important would have owned any kind of chair in this period. Medieval

[5] *Richter, pp. 97–116.*
[6] *Liversidge, pp. 11–34.*

6. Romano-British statue of a divinity, possibly Fortuna, seated in a low-backed wicker chair. Found at the fort of Birdoswald on Hadrian's Wall. Tullie House Museum, Carlisle

furnishings were sparse by our standards, but nevertheless contemporary documents and illustrations make it clear that relatively humble people had chairs in their own homes. This did not mean that they would be entitled to a chair at a public assembly, where the rules of social precedence created a hierarchy of seating. This took into account both comfort and the need for visibility: a chair with a back and arms ranked more highly than a bench or stool, which in its turn was preferable to sitting on the floor. Welsh bardic vocabularies, for instance, specify that at court 'the porch is for the yeomen, the step for the squires, the bench for the knights, and the *lleithig* [a low cushioned bench or stool] for the king'.[7] Within the confines of this hierarchy, further distinctions were marked not by the form of the seat itself, but rather by the other marks of estate which accompanied it. Most of these are already becoming familiar: the elevation of the seat on steps or a platform, the footstool, the use of symbolic decoration and precious materials. There was also an increased emphasis on rich textiles: the canopy, with its associated hangings, was a medieval introduction which proved of lasting significance (fig.7).

Few of the chairs in this book look especially comfortable to the modern eye. It would certainly be agonising to sit for very long in some of

[7] *Quoted in Peate. The first manuscripts of the vocabularies date from the fifteenth century, but he claims that they are 'demonstrably copies from earlier sources'.*

7. Design for a papal chair with an elaborate canopy by the architect Charles Heathcot Tatham. Pencil and watercolour, dated Rome 1794. E.372–1929

the commemorative chairs discussed in chapter V, especially the nineteenth-century exhibition pieces (fig.8). Yet the idea of comfort is inherent in the concept of the chair of authority, and is reflected in some of its distinguishing features. After all, its occupant may well be confined to it for several hours at a stretch. It is important to remember that loose cushions and draperies often replaced or supplemented fixed upholstery, which in any case has rarely survived in its original form. Moreover, portraits and other evidence suggest that people have not always sat in the same way. Changes in manners and deportment, and even the constraints created by dress, may alter our ideas of what constitutes a comfortable seat. Even so, some makers clearly miscalculated. In 1869 the chairmaker and town councillor Edwin Skull presented the corporation of High Wycombe with a 'handsome chair', intended for the use of the mayor (fig.9). A few years later, in 1877, his fellow councillor G. Wheeler as mayor 'found from presiding at a Public Meeting how uncomfortable the chairman's seat was' and replaced it with a new example.[8]

The ceremonial chair in Great Britain

No general study of seating of this kind in Great Britain has appeared before. A collection of material which Ambrose Heal gathered but never

THE "REPOSE" ARMCHAIR.—DESIGNED AND MODELED BY THOMAS.

8. The 'Repose' chair. Made by J. Thomas, with figures by Horsley, and shown at the Free Exhibition of Select British Manufactures in 1848. The carved decoration suggests the restfulness promised in its title in symbolic rather than real terms. Heal archive

published in the late nineteenth century is a partial exception which proved a useful source.[9] Otherwise, the subject has received some treatment in books dealing with chairs or furniture in general, and various individual chairs or groups of chairs have also been written up. The omission seems surprising. The subject has its own intrinsic interest, especially for a nation so preoccupied with tradition as the British.[10] It also has many implications for the more general study of furniture history. Chairs of this kind have usually been made with care, used infrequently, and cherished for posterity. Although they were made in far smaller numbers than ordinary domestic seating, they have a better survival rate. Moreover, the individuals and institutions who commissioned ceremonial chairs frequently kept records of their transactions. It is therefore often possible to establish a date and maker for these chairs, and other circumstances surrounding their manufacture. This is in contrast to the very high proportion of British furniture, even in public collections, which is unmarked and anonymous. Securely dated and provenanced examples have a special importance, and this study concentrates on them whenever possible. Obviously, the survival rate improves as one approaches the present day: genuine medieval examples are scarce, and have been eked out

[9] *Heal.*

[10] *For a stimulating analysis of the relationship between tradition and authority in Great Britain, and more particularly of the 'manufacture' of tradition during the last two centuries, cf. Hobsbawm & Ranger.*

9. Mayoral chair of the former borough of Chepping Wycombe, made and presented by Edwin Skull of High Wycombe in 1869. Replaced eight years later because it was so uncomfortable. Guildhall Heritage Exhibition, High Wycombe

here with contemporary illustrations, some of which come from further afield. The situation improves for the seventeenth and eighteenth centuries, and there is almost too much material for the nineteenth century, which may be described as the golden age of the ceremonial and commemorative chair. Here in particular it was necessary to pick and choose, rather than attempt a comprehensive survey.

This study is organised thematically, but its chapters also reflect the chronology of surviving examples. The earliest remaining British ceremonial chairs are ecclesiastical and royal, while the chairs of official bodies and societies are mainly post-medieval, and the idea of commemorative or relic chairs can only be traced back as far as the seventeenth century. A final chapter considers the ceremonial chair in the twentieth century. Some examples are the work of well-known designers and makers. Others are the first pieces to be attributed to more obscure figures. The best of them unite elegance with magnificence, but it has to be said that some of the others only manage to combine pomposity with banality. In between these two extremes, the aim is to include the eccentric and the entertaining, and to give some idea of the representative.

It seemed important to examine the way in which these chairs were commissioned and designed, wherever the documentation survived. Some

10. Portrait of Martin Folkes, President of the Royal Society between 1741 and 1752. Engraving by James Macardell after Thomas Hudson. 22234

11. The President's Chair of the Royal Society. English, about 1730. This shows the chair in fig. 10 as it is today. It appears in many other portraits of past presidents, including one of Sir Hans Sloane in the National Portrait Gallery dated 1736. Although it has been reupholstered many times and has lost its carved cresting, it is still used for its original purpose

12. *The Pope's Manhood declar'd in the Porphery Chair*. Early eighteenth-century engraving by B.Cole. According to an account in the *Gentleman's Magazine*, May 1732 'of all *Ecclesiasticall Chairs*, the *Apostolical* at *Rome*, is the most extraordinary, having in its Seat a Hole like a Close-Stool, through which two of the most eminent Cardinals examine the Person elected *Pope*, before he is confirm'd in his office'

13. *Sedes Busbiana*. Print published by Laurie and Whittle of Fleet Street in 1802. Dr Richard Busby was headmaster of Westminster School from 1638 until 1695, and this satirical print refers to his notorious reliance on the birch. It is said to be based on a painting by Sir Peter Lely presented to Dr Busby by Charles II, though the portrait in the centre is of his successor Dr South. 25016.634

preoccupations emerged as constant, and clearly the most important was the desire to create a display which would impress the beholder. Unfortunately, this is a difficult effect to convey on the printed page. Not all these chairs survive in the settings for which they were intended, and even fewer retain their original upholstery, hangings and other accessories. Out of context, they may look shabby or even faintly ludicrous. The use of contemporary illustrations helps circumvent this difficulty (figs.10,11). We may encounter more stubborn problems in identifying the purposes for which these chairs were intended (figs.12,13), and the symbolism which characterises much of their decoration (figs.14,15). Compared to our ancestors, we are visual illiterates in these matters: many of the details which simply appear magnificent or picturesque to our eyes were for them a very precise kind of visual shorthand, capable of conveying complex ideas about the user's possessions and pretensions vividly and immediately. Laborious explanations tend to spoil the effect.

Ceremonial chairs have their peculiar – at times very peculiar – stylistic

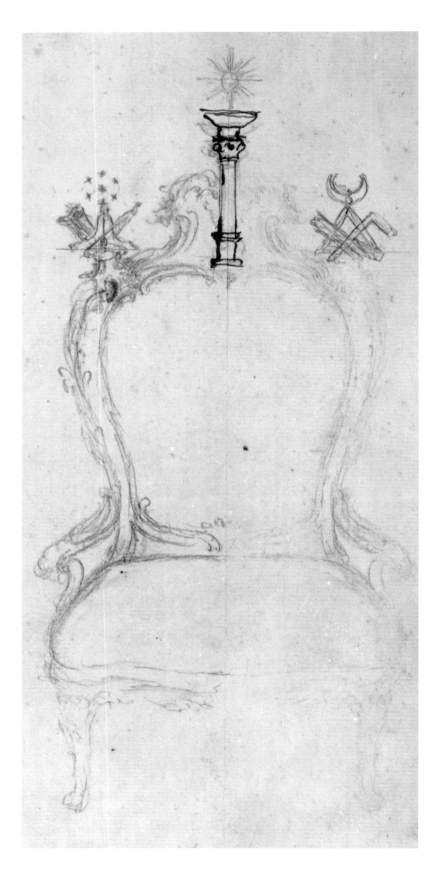

14. Design for a ceremonial chair. Matthias Lock, about 1740. The symbols decorating the back of this rococo chair indicate that it was intended for masonic use: each has a clear symbolic significance for those initiated in the laws of Freemasonry. 2848.146

15. Design for a ceremonial chair. Anonymous British watercolour of about 1780. The dolphin and mermaid motifs used in an accompanying decorative scheme suggest a marine connection, but the purpose of the chair itself, and its accompanying table, remain unclear. D.1277–1898

history, and some indications of this should emerge in the following chapters. From the late medieval period onwards, the majority of examples are enlarged versions of domestic armchairs, incorporating appropriate symbolic decoration. This is usually concentrated on the back of the chair, which will often be exceptionally high. Such a design has inherent problems of scale and proportion, and some of the examples illustrated in this study show that in inexperienced or uninspired hands these could all too easily become overwhelming. It should be apparent by now that the designer of a ceremonial chair worked within certain limitations defined by tradition, as well as practicality. Yet within these limitations there were no stylistic constraints, and no need to disregard fashion. Nevertheless, examples which can be precisely dated sometimes look rather old-fashioned, and it is interesting to speculate on the reasons for this. Before the nineteenth century it seems to have been largely a question of accidental survival rather than deliberate revival. The problem is discussed in chapter IV, where some of the officials' chairs which are illustrated look as if they were made about twenty or thirty years earlier than was actually the case. It is hard to believe that this was a deliberate choice, since other examples show that with a little more care or expense it was perfectly possible to create something up to date. The conscious selection of archaic forms and styles is a rather different matter, and it should become clear that this was a largely nineteenth-century phenomenon, influenced by the fashion for antiquarian furnishings as well as a more general interest in reviving past styles. Barry and Pugin's Gothic throne for the House of Lords, discussed in chapter III, is perhaps the most prominent illustration of a new feeling that a historic style was the most appropriate choice for a chair designed to convey authority. It is an attitude which has continued to dominate the design of ceremonial chairs ever since.

CHAPTER II

CATHEDRALS AND CHURCHES

All church seating is ceremonial, in the sense that both priest and worshippers have their appointed parts to perform in the service. Yet the clergy had permanent seats in church, which symbolised the sanctified authority of their office, long before any arrangements were thought necessary for the laity. This chapter concentrates on seating intended for presiding members of the clergy, since this expresses the concept of authority most clearly: thus bishops' thrones are included, but not choir stalls. In more recent times distinctive seating has also been set aside for certain lay officials, and this will also be considered. The chapter is divided into sections on fixed seating (which includes the earliest examples) and movable chairs. Most of the Post-Reformation examples are drawn from the Church of England, although it should be borne in mind that the apostolic tradition has ensured a good deal of common ground between Anglican and Roman Catholic usage. The Nonconformists' emphasis on the doctrine of equality before God would seem to make their places of worship an unrewarding area for study, although in some cases special seating might be provided for the minister or elders.[1]

16. 'St Wilfrid's throne'. Late seventh-century stone seat with incised ornament at Hexham Priory, Northumberland. From J. Charles Cox and Alfred Harvey, *English Church Furniture*, 1908

Fixed seating

The later Roman emperors handed over a number of basilicas for Christian worship. These were rectangular colonnaded halls intended for public assemblies or courts of justice, with a raised platform or tribunal in an apse at one end where the judge and his assessors sat. It was obviously convenient for Christians to adopt the same arrangement, both in these basilicas and in new churches built to the same plan. Traditionally therefore the clergy sat behind the altar facing the congregation, on a semicircle of seating running round the apse which was known as the *synthronon*. At its centre was the *cathedra*, a raised seat with back and arms which the bishop or abbot used to deliver his sermons and administer ecclesiastical law. Originally, the word *cathedra* simply signified a domestic armchair, but it was increasingly associated with a professor's or judge's chair, and eventually came to indicate the office itself. The same process of metonymy (the substitution of the name of an attribute or adjunct for that of the thing under discussion) is evident in the English words *see* and *cathedral*. The earliest surviving seats in English churches are made of stone and would probably originally have formed part of a synthronon. They appear very plain beside later bishops' thrones, though some have traces of decoration. One of the best preserved is carved with mouldings and interlace ornament (fig.16). This is traditionally described as the 'throne of St Wilfrid', who built Hexham church as his cathedral in the late seventh century. Its tub-like shape derives from Roman tradition, and recalls some of the Romano-British seats mentioned in chapter I. The likeness is even more pronounced in the case of a very plain stone chair in Beverley Minster.[2] Both these seats also came to serve as 'frithstols' (freed stools), in which a fugitive could seat himself to obtain the right of sanctuary.

This suggests that the venerable associations of these seats enhanced and authenticated their authority, giving them something of the status of holy relics. An even clearer indication of such a process survives at Norwich Cathedral, where three arms from a synthronon have been re-used in a

[1] *The Wycombe Chair Museum, for instance, has a presentation armchair given to the West Wycombe Methodist chapel in 1895 by Benjamin North, a local chair manufacturer. A chair in the Bunyan Meeting Library and Museum, Bedford, which is said to have belonged to John Bunyan, belongs rather with the relic chairs discussed in chapter V.*

[2] *Illustrated in Bond, p. 106.*

17. 'St Augustine's seat'. Thirteenth-century Purbeck marble archiepiscopal throne in Canterbury Cathedral. From J. Charles Cox and Alfred Harvey, *English Church Furniture*, 1908

stone bishop's throne behind the high altar, now heavily restored. The site of this see moved several times in the early middle ages, and the fragments probably came from Thetford when the final translation took place in 1094. They may go back to a still earlier site, perhaps the eighth-century cathedral at North Elmham or even the one built in the mid-seventh century at Dommoc. Evidently the reuse of these fragments was felt to provide continuity and thus legitimate the bishop's authority: further reinforcement was provided by a shaft beneath his feet, linking them to an arch beneath the throne containing holy relics.[3] A Purbeck marble throne behind the high altar at Canterbury Cathedral has traditionally been associated with its founder, St Augustine, though it probably dates from the thirteenth century (fig.17). The bishop's throne was not invariably placed behind the altar. An earlier throne at Canterbury before the Conquest is known to have been situated at the west end of the cathedral. Many early churches were oriented to the west, and this may indicate a survival of such an arrangement, or it may have been moved there in the tenth or eleventh century to reflect contemporary Carolingian practice (fig.45).

Later in the middle ages the area behind the altar was usually blocked off by tall retables and shrines, making the traditional position of the clergy increasingly impractical. They moved west into the choir, and the bishop's throne was placed on the south side of the stalls, at the east end next to the altar. Even at Canterbury the Archbishop normally sat on a wooden seat in the choir, and by the fifteenth century the marble seat was only used at his enthronement.[4] The change of position was accompanied by a change in style, as surviving fourteenth-century thrones demonstrate. The throne is

[3] *Radford, and A.B. Whittingham, 'Norwich Saxon Throne', Archaeological Journal, vol. cxxxvi (1979), pp. 60–8.*

[4] *Radford, pp. 126–8.*

18. Bishop's throne, Exeter Cathedral. Oak, about 1312–17, probably designed by Thomas of Winton. Engraving by H. le Keux after H. Shaw in John Britton, *The History and Antiquities of the Cathedral Church of Exeter*, London, 1826

transformed from a low stone chair into an elaborate architectural edifice, distinguished from the neighbouring choir stalls by its size and surmounting canopy. Like the holy relics in the tabernacle shrines which became popular around the same time, the bishop and his chaplains were enclosed in a soaring Gothic structure which both safeguarded them and emphasised their importance. There are also parallels with the wood and textile canopies which had become an important element in secular displays of authority, and which are discussed in the next chapter. The most spectacular surviving example of such a throne is the wooden example at Exeter (fig.18). Some 47 feet high, it was built during the incumbency of Bishop Stapleton (1308–27). The design is attributed to Thomas of Winton (Winchester), who is known to have visited Exeter for a month in 1313, and it is thought to have been completed in 1316 or 1317.[5] There are simpler examples at St David's and Hereford, and a stone screen-throne at Durham Cathedral, built above the chantry of Bishop Hatfield, after 1363. The south side of the east end was also the normal position for the *sedilia* found in some parish churches and cathedrals, which were usually made in groups of three, and were intended for the use

[5] *Bond, pp. 107–8, and Nikolaus Pevsner, The Buildings of England: South Devon, Harmondsworth, Penguin, 1952, p. 142.*

19. Sedilia at St Thomas, Winchelsea. Early fourteenth century, with an attached piscina or basin for washing the communion vessels. From W.D. Cooper, *History of Winchelsea*, London, 1850

of the officiating clergy during certain parts of the eucharist. Some were movable, but surviving examples are usually made of stone and recessed into niches in the wall. Often the one for the celebrant is at a higher level than those for the epistoler and gospeller, though this is not the case with the Decorated Gothic examples at Winchelsea (fig.19).

The east end of the southern range of choir stalls has remained the standard position for the *cathedra*, although adjustments to the accommodation sometimes proved necessary after the Reformation. When Cosimo, Grand Duke of Tuscany, attended a service at Exeter Cathedral in 1669 he was surprised to find the bishop's wife and nine children standing in a wooden enclosure at the foot of the throne.[6] The bishop's stall at St Paul's (fig.20) was carved by Grinling Gibbons and his assistants in 1696–7, and is covered by a canopy supported on Corinthian columns, richly carved with swags of flowers, leaves and ribbons. The surviving bills and sketches for some of the details in the cathedral library show that it was originally hung with velvet curtains, as shown in fig.21.[7] Few eighteenth- and early nineteenth-century thrones survive, apart from a throne at Winchester made by Garbett in about 1820. An example at Canterbury presented by Archbishop Tenison in 1704 stood under a *baldacchino* and was evidently influenced by Roman Baroque examples. Only the canopy survives, in another position. The Victorians tended to tidy away arrangements of this kind in favour of the correct but rather dull Gothic Revival replacements which can still be seen in many cathedrals. At Chester, for instance, Sir George Gilbert Scott was horrified to find that the substructure of the medieval shrine of St Werburgh had been commandeered for the bishop's throne. He reassembled the shrine and had a new throne made to his designs by Farmer and Brindley in 1876.[8]

Benches for the laity only began to appear in the fourteenth century, though people of importance no doubt made their own arrangements before this. These might be permanent and imposing in their private chapel or place of regular worship, like the 'well and suitably wainscotted and . . . painted' stalls to be provided for the king and queen in the church of St Peter at the Tower of London in 1240.[9] Private pews or 'close seats' for the wealthy are first mentioned in the late medieval period. The idea

[6] Travels of Cosmo the Third, Grand Duke of Tuscany, *London, J. Mawman, 1821, p. 130.*

[7] Wren Society, *vols. ii, pl. 29, xv, p. 192.*

[8] *David Cole*, The Work of Sir Gilbert Scott, *London, The Architectural Press, 1980, p. 91.*

[9] *Eames 1977, p. 203.*

20. The Bishop's Throne at St Paul's Cathedral, London. Carved by Grinling Gibbons in 1696–7. From Albert E.Bullock, *Grinling Gibbons and his compeers*, London, 1914

21. A service of thanksgiving for the recovery of George III at St Paul's Cathedral on 23 April 1789. Aquatint with etching by R. Pollard after E. Dayes. This gives a good view of the choir before the substantial alterations of the nineteenth century. The Bishop's and Lord Mayor's stalls are visible on the left, and there are further stalls for the Dean and the Bishop's domestic use on the right. Members of the royal family sit under a canopy erected for the occasion below the organ. 25844.2

22. Arthur Onslow, Speaker of the House of Commons, in his pew at St Margaret's, Westminster. Frontispiece of Thomas Wilson, *The Ornaments of Churches Considered*, 1761

spread rapidly in the sixteenth century. Box-pews could be furnished or rebuilt to meet individual requirements: at Northorpe Church in Lincolnshire the family at the Hall even had an extra one to accommodate their dogs until the early nineteenth century.[10] The local squire's pew was frequently decorated with his coat of arms, and elevated or otherwise distinguished architecturally from the rest. Similarly, John Evelyn noted in his diary after attending a Roman Catholic service in the new chapel at Whitehall on 29 December 1686 that 'the throne where the King and Queen sit is very glorious, in a closet above, just opposite the altar'. Other pews in a parish church might be reserved for some special use, for instance by women being churched or those doing public penance, or by the churchwardens. The last may still be distinguished by the staffs of office placed beside them. Local officials like the mayor or the judge of assizes might also have their designated pews. Again, these would be in a prime position and were often elevated or otherwise distinguished architecturally. Surviving examples are mostly to be found in eighteenth- and early nineteenth-century town churches, but as early as 1590 there is a reference to 'a new pew for the lorde maior on the South side & est ende of the churche' of St Peter Chepe in the City of London. This was apparently further distinguished by heraldic decoration incorporating 'greene men' with shields and arrows.[11] Wren provided a distinctive stall in the choir at St Paul's for the Lord Mayor (fig.21). The Speaker's box-pew at St Margaret's, Westminster in 1761 is shown in fig.22. This was probably fitted out in 1758, when the House of Commons provided £4000 for 'new pewing and decorating the church'.[12] It is much larger than

[10] *Heales, vol. i, pp. 144–5.*
[11] *Heales, vol i, p. 143.*
[12] *Mackenzie Edward Charles Walcott*, The History of the parish church of Saint Margaret in Westminster, *London, privately published, 1847, p. 12.*

Left:

23. The Adoration. Whalebone carving, perhaps a portable votive image. North-west Spanish, about 1100–50. Note the Virgin's footstool, and the canopy fixed to the arch above her head. 142–1866

Right:

24. Christ in Majesty. Embroidered silk twill panel from a cope. English, 1300–20. He sits on a cushioned stool within a Gothic niche, ornamented with the sun and moon and royal lions. T.337–1921

neighbouring pews, and crowned posts support curtains which screen the Speaker from draughts and curious eyes. The high-backed seat raised on a step is not unlike his official Chair in the House of Commons (fig.79). It includes a peg for his hat. Even a purely convivial organisation might set up an official pew. The Mock Corporation of Sefton, a dining and drinking club founded around 1764, had its own pew with three rows of seats and a square box for the 'mayor' in Sefton Church. Members would drive out from Liverpool for Sunday morning service, dine nearby at the Punch Bowl Inn, and then attend Evensong.[13]

Movable seating

Chairs as well as fixed seats can of course be used to denote authority, and they have the advantage that they can be moved around to meet different liturgical needs. Most of the rare examples of medieval chairs of state which survive are to be found in churches. Supported by contemporary inventories and illustrations (figs.23–6), these suggest the wide range of types in use. A rough-looking boarded armchair at St James's, Stanford Bishop, Herefordshire would presumably have been draped with textiles when in use (fig.27). It originally had an integral footboard, and its knockdown construction would have made it readily transportable. It is difficult to date so astylar an object, but a suggestion that it dates from the twelfth century certainly seems more credible than the traditional claim that it was used by St Augustine at a conference in 603.[14] The same problem arises in the association with the Venerable Bede, who died in 742, of an even more primitive-looking chair at Jarrow (fig.28). Chairs of

[13] *W.D. Caröe and E.J.A. Gordon,* Sefton, *London, Longmans Green & Co., 1893, ch. vi.*
[14] *Eames 1977, pp. 211–2.*

25. Panel from the Syon Cope. Embroidered linen, English, 1300–20. Christ and the Virgin sit on individual cushions on a long arcaded bench. 83–1864

state made from turned posts are frequently shown in medieval illustrations, and a rare example survives at Hereford Cathedral (fig.29). This was traditionally associated with King Stephen (ruled 1135–54) but is now usually dated around 1200. The type was certainly known earlier (fig.30). It originally had a footboard, and some of the posts from the back are missing: traces of the vermilion and gold paint which formed its original decoration were still visible in the nineteenth century.[15]

Chairs and stools with decorated metal frames were evidently popular. These would have been of the folding x-frame type discussed in chapter III. There were five iron chairs at St Paul's Cathedral in the thirteenth century, including 'a bishop's seat of silvered iron, with gilded human heads, which Bishop F. had'. This was given by Dean de Lucy, who died in 1241. An inventory of the vestry at Westminster Abbey in 1388 mentions 'three bishops' seats, one being silvered, the second and third iron, and three cloths for the same seats'.[16] There are no surviving examples of this type, but the battered remains of English x-chairs with wooden frames still survive in two cathedrals. One at Winchester has associations with the marriage of Queen Mary in 1554 and will be discussed in the next chapter (fig.56). The example at York Minster probably also dates from the mid-sixteenth century and has been associated with the enthronement of archbishops since at least the seventeenth century (fig.31).[17] Recent conservation showed that it was originally

[15] Eames 1977, pp. 210–11, and F.W. Havergal, Fasti Herefordenses, *illustrated by* G.C. Haddon, Edinburgh, R. Clark, 1869, pp. 123–8, pl. vi.

[16] Eames 1977, pp. 184–5.

[17] Eric C. Milnes, 'From rags to riches: a new look at an old chair', Furniture History, vol. xvii (1981), pp. 61–4.

26. The Coronation of the Virgin. Illumination from a book of hours produced in Paris in about 1400. Note the textiles used to drape the chair, and the canopy embroidered with stars. AL1646–1907

27. Boarded oak chair of state in St James's, Stanford Bishop, Herefordshire. Traditionally associated with St Augustine; possibly twelfth century. Cox and Harvey, *English Church Furniture*, 1908

upholstered with yellow silk velvet and fringing attached with gilt-headed nails, and could be at least partially folded up.[18]

From the nineteenth century onwards, one often comes across references to 'Glastonbury chairs' in churches and other settings. These will usually be reproductions of one or other of two chairs in the Bishop's Palace at Wells which are supposed to have associations with Glastonbury Abbey. Perhaps the more familiar is the folding chair with a laterally oriented x-frame which bears a Latin inscription referring to 'John Arthur, Monk of Glastonbury'. This is presumed to have belonged to John Arthur Thorne, the last Treasurer of Glastonbury Abbey. The distinctive simplicity of its design, combined with its romantic associations, has ensured that it has been widely reproduced since it was first published by Shaw in 1836 (fig.32). There seems no reason to doubt that it is a genuine early sixteenth-century chair: other examples of the type have been recorded, for instance the 'Prior's Chair' formerly at Southwick Priory, Hampshire (fig.33). The other 'Glastonbury Chair' is a much more elaborate turned

[18] Caroline Rendall, 'The Archbishop's chair – York Minster', in post-prints of a conference on the conservation of furnishing textiles held by the Scottish Society for Conservation and Restoration at the Burrell Collection, Glasgow, in March 1990.

28. Chair in Jarrow Church, traditionally associated with the Venerable Bede. Possibly fourteenth century. William B. Scott, *Antiquarian Gleamings in the North of England*, London, 1849

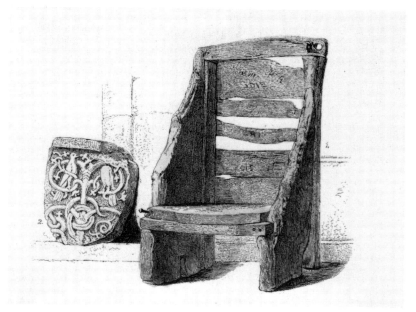

29. 'King Stephen's throne'. Turned chair of state in Hereford Cathedral, probably about 1200. Oak, originally painted. Illustration by G.C. Haddon from F.W. Havergal, *Fasti Herefordenses*, Edinburgh, 1869

30. The Adoration. German (Cologne), 1125–50. Walrus ivory plaque, probably from an altar frontal or pulpit. The Virgin is seated on a turned chair very like the Hereford throne. 145–1866

31. X-framed chair of state in York Minster. English, mid-sixteenth century. From Henry Shaw, *Specimens of Ancient Furniture*, London, 1836

32. Folding oak chair in the Bishop's Palace at Wells, early sixteenth century. The seat and base are restorations. Associated with John Arthur Thorne, the last Treasurer of Glastonbury Abbey. Henry Shaw, *Specimens of Ancient Furniture*, London, 1836

33. Anonymous engraving of the 'Prior's Chair', formerly in Southwick Priory, Hampshire. This appears to be an early sixteenth-century chair of the Glastonbury type. Heal Archive

34. Copy of a turned chair in the Bishop's Palace at Wells, traditionally associated with the last Abbot of Glastonbury. English, about 1830–40, ash and oak. W.24–1913

35. Bishop's chair, with the arms of Henry Compton, Bishop of London from 1675 to 1713. Probably supplied by John Bernard in 1697–9. Both the back and the seat were originally caned and there is evidence that heavy use has resulted in other alterations, notably to the legs. St Paul's Cathedral, London

armchair which is supposed to have belonged to the last Abbot, Richard Whiting. Abbot Whiting was executed by Henry VIII in 1539, but there is now general agreement that chairs of this type were not produced until the seventeenth century. It also seems that they were made to furnish provincial farmhouses, not to be used as chairs of state. Nevertheless, this chair has to some extent a prior claim to the 'Glastonbury Chair' title, as it was published some ten years earlier than the other in Richard Wright's *History of the Abbey of Glaston* (1826) and was also apparently being reproduced from an earlier date. An example in the V&A's collections may be one of the facsimile copies that the furniture broker Kensett of Mortimer Street was selling by 1835 (fig.34).[19] In the Great Exhibition of 1851, a furniture maker from Wells showed both a full-sized oak copy and a miniature ivory model.[20]

Surviving seventeenth- and eighteenth-century bishops' chairs conform to the usual pattern for officials' chairs at this date: they are large, high-

[19] *Wainwright, p. 59.*
[20] *See chapter V, p. 102.*

36. Painted sanctuary chair in Shobdon
Church, Herefordshire. About 1755

backed versions of contemporary domestic armchairs, with heraldic and
sacred ornament. At the Roman Catholic service in Whitehall Chapel in
1686 John Evelyn also noted that the bishop 'in his mitre and rich copes'
sat near the altar 'in a chair with armes pontificaly', which was presumably
of this type. A handsome chair used within the bishop's throne at St Paul's
bears the arms of Bishop Compton and was probably amongst the
furnishings for the choir area supplied by the upholsterer John Bernard
between 1697–9 (fig.35). Bernard's accounts mention four 'great chairs',
including two with 'frames of walnut finely carved'. Movable furniture was
also supplied for royal visitors on 'occasions of thanksgiving and other
solemnities', like the ceremony in fig.21. As much as £2000 was allowed
for a new set in 1722.[21] Bishops' mitres surmount a sturdy country-made
splat-backed armchair at Southwell Minster,[22] and a more sophisticated
upholstered armchair at Wells, both of which date from the mid-
eighteenth century.

One or more chairs are also often placed near the altar of a parish
church, the modern descendants of the sedilia mentioned above. The
bishop may use one of these on his occasional visits, or another special
chair may be provided for him. Few purpose-made examples predate the
nineteenth century, with rare exceptions like fig.36. This is one of two
sanctuary chairs which form part of the Gothick furnishings of Shobdon

[21] Wren Society, vol. xv, pp. 36–7, 42,
48, vol. xvi, pp. 111, 137.

[22] John T. Kirk, American furniture and
the British tradition to 1830, New York,
Alfred A. Knopf, 1982, no. 842.

37. The chapel of St John, St Mary's Church, Guildford. E.W. Brayley and J. Britton, *A Topographical History of Surrey*, Dorking, 1841

38. The 'Prior's Chair', Little Dunmow Church, Essex. Probably cut down from a set of thirteenth-century choir stalls. Fred Roe, *Old Oak Furniture*, London, 1905

39. The 'Abbot's chair' at Evesham. Partially fourteenth century. From Henry Shaw, *Specimens of Ancient Furniture*, London, 1836

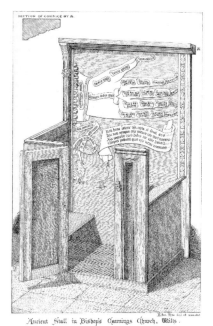

40. The 'Meditation Chair', Bishops Canning, Wiltshire. Illustration from the *Wiltshire Archaeological Society's Magazine*, 1860

23 *Gothick, exhibition at Brighton Royal Pavilion, Art Gallery & Museums, 1975*, cats. A25–8.

24 Roe, *pp. 86–7.*

25 *There are some grim examples of 'antiquarian' pieces in Bond, pp. 111–30, for instance.*

26 Country Life, *vol. cxix, no. 3099 (7 June 1956), p. 1237.*

Church in Herefordshire, built by John, 2nd Viscount Bateman in 1753.[23] Many more examples are obviously secular in origin and were probably originally introduced for a specific occasion like a bishop's visit. Thus an early eighteenth-century hall or porter's chair, decorated with casts of the Barrett family crest, at Aveley Church in Essex was probably introduced in 1799 by Lady Dacre, for the consecration of regimental colours which she had presented.[24]

Such a chair would not receive heavy use, and obviously did not have to be new when it arrived. It might well be that an older piece was not just easier to spare but was regarded as more suitable for such a setting and purpose. Certainly antiquarian fervour and the associated fashion for old oak tended to encourage this idea in the nineteenth century. It could have happy results. The chapel of St John at St Mary's, Guildford is shown being used as a lumber room in 1841 (fig.37). When the church was restored by Thomas Goodchild in 1863 it was cleared out, but the handsome seventeenth-century chair at the centre of the picture was retained for use in the chancel. In other cases the results were less fortunate, and the sanctuary area could all too easily become a kind of elephants' graveyard, silting up with chairs made up from old carvings and outright forgeries as well as genuinely old pieces.[25] Sometimes it was treated as a local history museum. A seventeenth-century chair at Sandal Church, West Yorkshire, was apparently purchased by the vicar for 'five golden guineas' from the nearby Three Houses Inn, on the grounds that the notorious highwayman Nick Nevison had been sitting in it when he was captured.[26] Perhaps the best-known of these antiquarian pieces is the 'Prior's Chair' at Little Dunmow, Essex,

41. Bishop's throne, probably designed by William Butterfield. Oak with painted polychrome decoration, about 1870. On loan to the V&A from All Saints' Church, Margaret Street, London

associated with the ceremony of the Dunmow Flitch (fig.38). Since 1445, a gammon of bacon has periodically been awarded to any married couple who can swear that they have not quarrelled for a year and a day. According to tradition, they were also 'chaired' in the 'prior's chair'. This is in fact the cut down remains of the end unit from a set of stalls, probably dating from the thirteenth century. By the mid-eighteenth century, the ceremony had fallen into abeyance, but the author Harrison Ainsworth revived it in 1855, a year after the publication of his popular novel, *The Flitch of Bacon*. The setting was moved to Great Dunmow, three miles away, and the chair was no longer used. It became a regular and popular event, despite some opposition from the local gentry and derision from more purist antiquarians.[27] A number of other cherished antiquarian pieces have evidently been cut down from stalls or other fixed furnishings, for instance the 'Abbot's chair' at Evesham (fig.39) and 'Edward I's chair' in the chapter house at Lincoln Cathedral (fig.4, bottom right), both heavily restored. The 'Meditation Chair' in fig.40 seems to have been cut down from a late medieval monastic carrel (an

[27] *Roe, pp. 62–4, and the same author's* Old Oak Furniture, *London, Methuen, 1908 (2nd edition), pp. 55–9.*

42. X-framed bishop's confirmation chair with bullock's hide upholstery. Supplied by Robert Christie of George Street, Portman Square for Truro Cathedral in 1888. Illustration from *The Cabinet Maker and Art Furnisher*, 1 November 1888

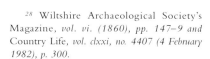

43. Oak sanctuary chair made for Ellesmere Church, Shropshire, by Mrs C. J. Eliot of Foleshill Vicarage, Coventry, Miss K. Sharp and Miss Edwards in 1890. Illustration from *The Cabinet Maker and Art Furnisher*, 1 April 1890

28 Wiltshire Archaeological Society's Magazine, *vol. vi. (1860), pp. 147–9 and* Country Life, *vol. clxxi, no. 4407 (4 February 1982), p. 300.*

29 Victorian Church Art, *Victoria and Albert Museum, 1971–2, catalogue no. C22.*

30 Cabinet Maker and Art Furnisher, *vol. ix, no. 101 (1 Nov. 1888), p. 129.*

31 *The Newsletter of the Ancient Monuments Society, summer 1992, recorded a Mr Gordon Browning as the one remaining maker. At this point he was 81 and looking for a successor.*

enclosed desk for private study). It may have been intended for sinners doing public penance, since it is decorated with a large hand bearing various pious warnings.[28]

When new chairs were needed, the Victorians again looked to the past. The Gothic style was especially popular, and is used in a simplified form for the bishop's throne shown in fig.41. This comes from the church of All Saints, Margaret Street, built by William Butterfield between 1849 and 1859. The throne is undocumented and did not form part of the original furnishings, but is thought to have been provided by Butterfield in the 1870s.[29] Its polychrome decoration is certainly in keeping with the rest of his work there. A more conventional chair provided for the bishop's use at confirmations in J.L.Pearson's cathedral at Truro is x-framed (fig.42),[30] while the influence of the Arts and Crafts movement is evident in the sanctuary chair shown in fig.43. Although the three women makers described it as 'in the style of the fourteenth century', it is a simple but obviously late nineteenth-century chair-form to which conventionalised Gothic foliage has been boldly applied. The *Cabinet Maker and Art Furnisher* somewhat patronisingly praised it for being 'altogether free from the finikin element which so frequently characterises carving coming from the hands of the fair sex'. Some stock patterns of the kind discussed in chapter IV were also intended for ecclesiastical use, and many may still be found in churches today. Reproductions of the folding Glastonbury chair discussed above (fig.32) were especially popular and are still being produced.[31]

CHAPTER III

ROYAL THRONES AND CHAIRS OF STATE

Much of the pageantry associated with medieval royalty still exists in an adapted form today, especially for state occasions like coronations. In some ways the survival of these traditional ceremonies makes it easy to forget that they originally served a very different kind of political purpose. The medieval monarch's authority was underlined by the use of symbolism and allegory, but it was very far from being merely symbolic. Ceremonial was simply the most vivid and effective means of mass communication available at a time when few people could read and write, but visual literacy was more highly developed. Rituals which now seem obscure or simply picturesque had a clear symbolic purpose, and amongst the key symbols of the monarch's authority was the throne.

Medieval coronations

The laws governing the succession to the throne have been clearly set out in modern times: a new monarch automatically steps into the place of the old one, and a coronation follows as a matter of course. An Anglo-Saxon or Norman king's powers were far greater, but the rules governing the succession were more fluid. He chose his successor from amongst his kin, but did not have to pick his eldest son or nearest male relative, if somebody else seemed more suitable. Contests usually arose when the position had not been clearly defined before his death: in 1066, for instance, and again in 1135. In these circumstances, the coronation ceremony could assume a critical importance in validating a new monarch's claim to the throne.

Unfortunately, the further back beyond the Norman Conquest we go the sketchier the evidence about coronations becomes. Some traces of older ceremonies survive. The election ceremonies of Germanic kings in the fifth and sixth centuries often culminated in the king being raised on a shield by his followers. While there is no evidence that this ceremony ever took place in this country, the Anglo-Saxon monarch did need to obtain the recognition of the *Witan*, or royal council. Some optimistic constitutional historians of the nineteenth century went so far as to claim that the *Witan* actually chose the ruler, but modern interpretation has tended to reduce its role to a formality.[1] The coronation service used to include a preliminary ceremony in Westminster Hall, where the monarch mounted a throne in the presence of his peers and officers of state, before setting off in procession to the abbey. This has not taken place since 1821, but a formal call for Recognition is still part of the service.[2]

The idea that a coronation should be a religious ceremony of dedication emerged in the eighth century. It was an imitation of developments on the Continent, where the Church had devised ceremonies to confirm the position of a new Frankish dynasty by drawing on Old Testament and Byzantine precedents. The Pope sanctioned the anointment and coronation of Pippin in 751, and personally anointed two sons of Charlemagne in 781. Through his anointment with oil and chrism, a procedure akin to the ordination of priests and the consecration of bishops, the monarch could claim spiritual as well as temporal authority. It was a crucial development. The first reliable reference to a Christian service in

[1] *See, for instance, Christopher Brooke,* The Saxon and Norman Kings, *London, Batsford, 1963, ch. ii.*
[2] *Tanner.*

44. The King's Stone. Grey wether sandstone block near the Guildhall at Kingston-on-Thames. The base and railings date from 1850, and were designed by Major Davis FSA

45. The throne of Charlemagne in Aachen Cathedral, Germany. Marble and oak on a limestone base. The iron mounts include hooks for textiles on the base. Ninth or tenth century

[3] *William A. Chaney,* The Cult of kingship in Anglo-Saxon England: the transition from paganism to Christianity, *Manchester, Manchester University Press, 1970, pp. 135–7.*

England comes in 787 when King Offa designated his son Ecgfrith as his heir by having him crowned and 'consecrated'. The first English coronation of which we have a detailed record is that of King Edgar at Bath in 973. This included anointment, enthronement and most of the other elements of the modern service.

The royal regalia, including the throne, seem to have become hallowed by use and considerable importance attached to their possession. We are told that Canute 'sat on the throne of the kingdom', for instance, after he triumphantly entered London in 1017. This attitude partly reflects the survival of pre-Christian cults of kingship.[3] There was a widespread and very ancient tradition of inaugurating a monarch by seating him on a sacred stone, and it has been claimed that the 'King's Stone' at Kingston-on-Thames (fig.44) was used for this purpose. Certainly at least five coronations in the tenth century were held at Kingston. An analogy can also be drawn between the royal throne and the bishop's *cathedra,* discussed in the last chapter. This is particularly evident in the case of the throne in Aachen Cathedral (fig.45). Whether or not this was installed by Charlemagne before he was buried there in 814, it was certainly in

LES: HIC DEDERVNT:HAROLDO: HIC RE SIDET:HAROLD
CORO   NA: REGIS   REX:AN   GLORVM:
STIGANT
ARCHIEPS

46. Detail from the Bayeux tapestry, showing the coronation of Harold in Westminster Abbey in 1066. It is doubtful whether this event actually took place. English or French, 1070s. Linen with wool embroidery

position for the coronation of Otto I in 936, and was subsequently used for the coronation of every German ruler up to and including Ferdinand I in 1531. It is placed at the west end of the cathedral in the gallery, raised on six steps like Solomon's throne. From this commanding position, far higher than that of bishop and priest, the occupant could both see and be seen everywhere in the cathedral. Its present appearance unfortunately owes a certain amount to nineteenth-century restoration, but it is clear that slabs of antique marble were re-used for its construction, and that it could be hung with textiles to enhance its somewhat austere appearance.[4]

Edward the Confessor sited his chief palace next door to Westminster Abbey and rebuilt the original monastery, attracted by the claim that it had been miraculously consecrated by St Peter. He was buried there soon after its reconsecration in 1065, and his own sanctity rapidly became an important element in its reputation. Harold may or may not have been crowned there (fig.46), but the coronation of William I on Christmas Day 1066 set a precedent which has remained unbroken to this day. After 1245, Henry III rebuilt the Abbey as a shrine to Edward, and a setting for royal ceremonial. The choir and choir stalls were left in the nave, creating a large area between the north and south transepts which could be built up with staging for coronations. This is now known as the Theatre, and is usually set at the level of the adjacent sanctuary. In the medieval period it was known as the Mount or Scaffold and was raised far higher to ensure visibility: at the coronation of Edward II in 1308, for instance, it was high enough for men on horseback to ride underneath without stooping.

By this date the ceremony had acquired an additional focus. Edward I had captured the Stone of Scone from the Scots in 1296. This block of sandstone was associated with the coronation of the Kings of Scotland, and there is some slight evidence to suggest that it has been cut down from a stone chair. The first written reference to it only goes back as far as 1249, but legend claimed it had been used as a pillow both by Jacob at Bethel and St Columba on Iona, and identified it with the Irish Stone of Destiny. It was therefore a powerful talisman, which Edward decided to place within a new coronation chair at Westminster Abbey, like the holy relics within an altar. He originally asked his goldsmith Adam to create a bronze chair, but in August 1297 work on this was abandoned for reasons of economy. The existing oak chair (fig.47) was supplied by Master Walter of Durham, the King's Sergeant Painter, between 1297 and 1300. It has been

[4] *Walter Maas, Der Aachener Dom, Cologne, Greven Verlag, 1984, pp. 27–30.*

47. The Coronation Chair, Westminster Abbey. Oak, made between 1297 and 1300 by Master Walter of Durham

used at every coronation since that of Edward II.[5] In a highly symbolic act the chair and stone were even taken to Westminster Hall for Oliver Cromwell's investiture as Lord Protector in 1657. A second, plainer chair of the same pattern was made for Mary II's joint coronation with William III in 1689: as she was several inches taller than her husband its seat is proportionally lower. Inevitably the chair has undergone many alterations and repairs over the centuries, of which it is only possible to mention the most important.[6] The original decorative scheme was highly architectural: crocketed pinnacles rose from the back and arms, and the sides, front and back were carved with shields, arcading and other Gothic motifs, with some painted and gilded decoration. Two small painted and gilded wooden leopards (a term used to describe lions in medieval heraldry) were separately supplied and may have been placed on the arms. In 1301 Master Walter also supplied a painted and gilded step and a protective case for the chair. The step, the lions and the predominantly white and gold colour scheme all recall once more the throne of Solomon. Some fifty years later much of this carved decoration was stripped off to make way for pounced

[5] *It is sometimes claimed that Queen Mary refused to sit in the chair because it had been 'polluted' by her Protestant brother Edward VI, but Tanner makes it clear that it was – unusually – used as the throne for the Homage, rather than the actual Coronation.*

[6] *For a full account see Percival-Prescott.*

gilding. The seated figure of a king was added inside the back, and foliage, birds, grotesques and small decorative patterns filled other areas. Only fragments of this scheme survive. The four supporting lions were probably added for Henry VIII's coronation in 1509, although documentary evidence suggests they are now replacements made in 1727.

Medieval thrones

A distinction needs to be drawn between the Coronation Chair and other kinds of royal thrones. The special purpose and associations of the Coronation Chair gave it the status of a relic, rather than a piece of furniture. Other royal thrones certainly drew on the same imagery, like the wooden seat which Henry III ordered for Westminster Hall in 1245. This was also flanked by lions, which were to have been of marble until the king decided gilt bronze would be 'more splendid'. There are also parallels for the image of the king inside the Coronation Chair, which clearly suggested an ever-watchful regal presence even in his absence. This motif was apparently reserved for seats permanently designated as thrones, like the seat made for Henry III's use at Windsor in 1250 which was decorated with the figure of a king holding a sceptre in his hand. A gilded copper statue of a king was also placed in an arch over the throne in Westminster Hall for Edward II's coronation feast in 1308. Other symbols could also indicate royal authority: at Winchester Henry III installed a bench and royal seat at the east end of the great hall, with a wheel of fortune painted in the gable above.[7]

However, most thrones were simply treated as furniture, and few seem to have been exclusively reserved for the monarch. As chapter I showed, there was a hierarchy of seating at any medieval assembly which entitled the most powerful person present to the best seat. It is therefore not surprising to find other people using seats of the same kind. Moreover, the king's deputy might legitimately use the king's seat. Westminster Hall, for instance, was not only the setting for coronation banquets and other state occasions, but also served as the home of three courts of justice – Common Pleas, King's Bench and Chancery. Early fourteenth-century inventories of its furnishings show that the Court of Chancery took place at the south end of the hall, where there was a raised dais with a marble chair and table. This was used by the king when he dined in state, and by the chancellor when the court was sitting. The other court furnishings were removable: elevated benches for the justices, with lower ones at their feet for their senior clerks. The litigants sat opposite on more benches, divided from the officials by a long table on trestles. Each court area was enclosed by bars made from oak planks.[8] This account also suggests the flexibility required of all kinds of medieval furniture, including seating. Each room and its furnishings needed to serve several functions. The court also needed to progress continually between different palaces and castles. Only items which could be fixed down or stored, or which were of small value in any case, could be safely left behind: everything else was taken along. Hence the emphasis on folding x-frame stools and chairs, discussed in the next section. Wooden furniture had little intrinsic value compared to plate and textiles, but even so there was an emphasis on mobility: trestle tables, benches, stools. Even something as primitive looking as the chair of state in fig.27 could be readily dismantled.

Contemporary illustrations show fixed seats, benches, settles, stools and chairs all being used in circumstances which suggest the authority of the sitter (figs.23–6, 46, 48–51). Even a single, relatively early source like the Bayeux tapestry includes a considerable variety of forms (figs.46, 48–50).[9] Most of these would have been made from wood or stone, precious

[7] HOKW, *vol. i, pp. 130, 506, 545. vol. ii, pp. 859, 868.*

[8] HOKW, *vol. i, pp. 543–5.*

[9] *A wide selection are sketched in Eames 1977, section D.*

Top:

48. Edward the Confessor in his palace at Westminster, from the Bayeux tapestry. He sits on a four-legged stool with a cushion and footstool, and what looks like a canopy over his head

49. Harold in conversation with William of Normandy, from the Bayeux tapestry. This stool is more like a chest in form, but is also decorated with animal heads and feet

[10] Mercer, p. 46.

materials usually being confined to x-framed seats. Some were traditional types which altered very little over hundreds of years, like the thrones made up from turned posts. No doubt many of these had painted decoration like the surviving example at Hereford (fig.29). Neither decorative technique required much skill, and as Mercer suggests this was probably one reason why they remained popular.[10] Other thrones, like the Coronation Chair, were more sophisticated interpretations of contemporary architectural fashions (fig.51). Chapter I outlined the hierarchy of forms in which a chair ranked more highly than a stool, but this only applied if both were present. It was the accompanying marks of estate, rather than the form of the seat itself, which symbolised the authority of its occupant. Such a seat would be placed in the most

commanding position in a room. It would probably be elevated on a dais or steps and might be further distinguished by painting or statuary. It usually had a footboard, or was accompanied by a footstool. Cushions and other textiles, of greater intrinsic value than the chair itself, would be used to dress it up. A new and important development in the later middle ages was the appearance of a canopy or cloth of estate above such a chair or over a state bed. The origins of this phenomenon are unclear, although historians have assumed that chair canopies derive from bed canopies.[11] The use of fixed wooden canopies appears to predate cloth ones in England: Henry III ordered a bed at Westminster in 1242–7 which had posts painted green and powdered with gold stars, and a painted canopy,

Top:

50. Harold seated on the throne of England, from the Bayeux tapestry. This seat has a high back decorated with monsters' heads

51. Engraving of some thirteenth- and fourteenth-century Great Seals of England, showing elaborately architectural chairs of state. From Paul de Rapin-Thoyras, *History of England*, 1729. Heal Archive

[11] *See Eames 1971, section B and Eames 1977.*

52. St Peter dictating the Gospel to St Mark. Ivory, South Italian (?), late eleventh century. Note the two laterally oriented x-frame chairs, one with dolphin arms. 270–1867

and a canopied throne for his hall at Woodstock in 1252.[12] The Gothic structures erected over bishops' thrones, like the fourteenth-century example at Exeter discussed in the last chapter (fig.18), represent the most extreme development of this type. In the end, however, the cloth canopy assumed the greater importance, presumably because it offered greater flexibility and better opportunities for display (figs.23, 26, 48).

X-framed chairs and stools

Throughout the breakup of the Roman Empire from the third century AD onwards, the folding stool or *sella curulis* associated with its magistrates and army commanders seems to have remained a potent symbol of authority in Europe. Hallowed by traditions stretching back to the ancient Near East, it was also easy to carry around, even on a military campaign. It could be made of wood or metal, usually iron. The form lent itself to rich decoration, sometimes in precious materials: elements of many examples terminated in animal or human heads which proved especially well suited to this treatment. The form was certainly used by Frankish rulers: a contemporary illumination shows Lothar I using an x-framed seat at his coronation in 843. A study devoted to the *sella curulis* through the ages has shown how the laterally oriented x-frame of the antique world

[12] HOKW, *vol. i, pp. 497–8, vol. ii, pp. 1010–1.*

53. Nineteenth-century electrotype copy of the 'Throne of Dagobert' in the Bibliothèque Nationale, Paris. The original gilded bronze stool probably dates from the late eighth century, and the back and arms from the second half of the ninth century. 1868–16

transformed itself into the frontally-oriented medieval faldstool around this point. The situation is not entirely clearcut, as the study itself includes a frontally-oriented Ancient Egyptian stool,[13] and laterally-oriented examples were still produced right through the middle ages (figs.32, 52). Its Carolingian associations certainly helped to surround the faldstool with a heroic glow in the later medieval imagination. For instance the eleventh-century *Chanson de Roland* describes Charlemagne at the siege of Cordova sitting on his golden faldstool in an orchard, surrounded by his entourage seated on white carpets. It also mentions an ivory faldstool used by his rival, the Saracen king Marsilion. The surviving 'Throne of Dagobert' (fig.53) is first mentioned amongst the treasures of the royal French abbey of Saint-Denis by the Abbot Suger around 1151: he believed it to be the throne the Frankish kings customarily used to receive the first homage of their nobles. The throne was clearly originally a faldstool, to which a back and arms were added on. These echo the form of St Peter's chair in Rome, suggesting perhaps the combination of temporal and spiritual authority (fig.54).[14]

As we saw in chapter II, x-framed seats were used in churches as well as palaces. They were both convenient and relatively comfortable, and some medieval illustrations show them being used for purely practical purposes

[13] *Wanscher, p. 66.*
[14] *cat. no. 5 in* Le Trésor de Saint-Denis, *Musée du Louvre, Paris, March–June 1991.*

54. The chair of St Peter. About AD 843; the ivory plaques were added later. The chair is now encased inside Bernini's baroque reliquary-throne in St Peter's, Rome. From Arthur Ashpitel and Alexander Nesbitt, *Saint Peter's Chair*, London, 1870

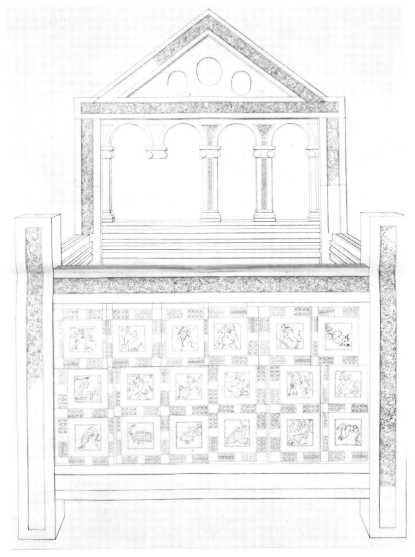

55. X-framed folding stool, probably twelfth-century Byzantine. Iron inlaid with copper and silver. The seat cover is not original. 696–1904

56. X-framed chair at Winchester Cathedral, associated with Queen Mary's wedding in 1554. Oak frame with blue velvet upholstery, fixed with gilded nails. The gilded copper finials are engraved with the letters IHS, and repoussé copper plaques cover the x-join

with no ceremonial overtones: for the dressing of hair or wounds, for instance.[15] Faldstools had a fabric or leather seat, very like today's campstool (fig.55). X-framed chairs also lent themselves to more ambitious experiments in upholstery. Although they are more cumbersome, many examples were still designed to fold up like a pair of scissors. Often the frame would be constructed in this way although fixed seat and back rails were then attached. This is true even of a seventeenth-century example like the Juxon chair. Sometimes a leather seat was slung from the arms to form a kind of hammock. From the mid-fifteenth century the whole wooden frame, as well as the seat and back, might be covered in fabric, fixed into place with gilded nails.[16] A surviving armchair of this type at Winchester Cathedral is associated with the marriage of Queen Mary in 1554 (fig.56) and is not unlike the example at York shown in fig.31. This is made to fold: the seat cushion rests on webbing, and the webbing visible on the back would originally have been mounted with velvet. X-framed chairs of state appear in many sixteenth- and seventeenth-century portraits, usually frustratingly half-hidden by the sitter (fig.57). No fewer than eleven can be glimpsed in the painting of the English and Spanish delegates at the 1604 Somerset House peace conference (fig.58). It is striking confirmation that these chairs of state were not the exclusive preserve of the monarch. Despite their family resemblance, the chairs are upholstered in different colours – predominantly red and blue – and are in no way a matched set. Perhaps

57. Portrait of Edward VI. English School, about 1547. The king stands in front of an x-framed chair upholstered in green velvet with gilded lions' legs and pommels. Note the oriental carpet and the silk canopy, which would have resembled that shown in fig.26. National Portrait Gallery

[15] *Eames 1977, p. 184.*
[16] *Symonds.*

58. *The Somerset House peace conference*, 1604. Oil on canvas, by an unknown artist. National Portrait Gallery

they had been issued to the delegates individually, like the sets of state furniture for ambassadors mentioned below.

After about 1600, the x-framed chair seems simply to have failed to develop any further, either stylistically or constructionally. Magnificent but unwieldy, it was gradually superseded by other less cumbersome forms of upholstered seating and had virtually disappeared by the end of the seventeenth century. A well-known collection of state furniture at Knole was brought to the house in 1701 by the 6th Earl of Dorset, who had been William III's Lord Chamberlain from 1689 to 1697, and was entitled to outmoded or outworn royal furnishings by virtue of his office.[17] Some, but not all, of the chairs are x-framed: the best preserved of those that are is upholstered in red velvet and bears a stencil indicating that it was being used at Hampton Court in 1661. A very similar armchair in the V&A also dates from the mid-seventeenth century (fig.59). It has a firm connection with William Juxon, Archbishop of Canterbury (1582–1663), but other stories which circulated when it first appeared in print at the end of the eighteenth century are romantic inventions of a kind which will appear again in chapter V. The most sensational and characteristic was the claim that it was used on the scaffold at Charles I's execution in 1649. Spots of blood on the velvet upholstery were offered as corroboration, but no trace of these can be found. Less spectacularly but with no more evidence, it was suggested that the chair was used at Charles I's trial, or at Charles II's coronation in 1661.[18] Recent conservation has restored some of its original splendour. The purple velvet upholstery was originally of two distinct

[17] *Jackson-Stops.*
[18] *For fuller details see in the bibliography under (Juxon chair).*

59. The Juxon chair and stool. Beechwood frame with velvet upholstery; about 1630–60. W12 & 13–1928

shades, and both the fringing and nail-heads were gilded. It is interesting to note that the back was covered in a greeny-blue satin, perhaps for reasons of economy as this area would not normally be seen.

The footstool which accompanies the Juxon chair has clearly been cut down. It was perhaps originally one of a much higher pair of flanking side stools, intended for the display of regalia rather than seating. A footstool would have been required as well to make up the formal suite of furnishings known as a 'state', which would also have included a canopy and its hangings and a carpet. The Commonwealth inventories of Charles I's possessions include many states. Some were valued at as much as £100, because of the rich textiles: one embellished with pearls and precious or semi-precious stones reached £500.[19] Some of the chairs at Knole are still accompanied by stools, while the Spangled Bed probably originally formed a canopy for the seat furniture in the same set. The Commonwealth inventories include some variations on the standard set. For instance, double-ended couches were for formal use under a canopy, not for relaxation. One survives at Knole: others have rather misleadingly been converted into 'daybeds' by removing one end.[20]

From the Restoration to the nineteenth century

The rich display of textiles associated with the medieval throne thus remained an essential feature of the baroque state apartment, and for the same reasons.[21] Describing a green velvet state embroidered with gold and silver in the Drawing Room at Windsor in 1698, Celia Fiennes somewhat grudgingly conceded that 'it looked very glorious, and was newly made to give audience to the French Ambassador to show the grandeur and magnificence of the British monarch – some of these fooleries are requisite

[19] *Jervis, pp. 289–90.*
[20] *Thornton.*
[21] *Baillie.*

60. The Enthronement of James II and Mary in 1685. Anonymous engraving from Francis Sandford, *History of the Coronation of James II and Queen Mary*, 1687. E.814–1959

22 *Christopher Morris*, The Journeys of Celia Fiennes, *London, Cresset Press, 1947, p. 280.*

23 HOKW, *vol. v, pp. 274, 324, 326–7.*

24 General Evening Post, *Sept 14–6, 1735*

sometimes to create admiration and regard to keep up the state of a kingdom and nation'.[22] Other thrones apparently had a more permanent architectural framework, though they may still have been used in conjunction with hangings and movable chairs. The throne constructed for Charles II in St George's Hall at Windsor was evidently elaborately allegorical, although its exact appearance is unknown. It was supported on six slaves and included figures of Prudence and Justice and three Fames, carved by Lewis Vanupstall and John Vanderstaine for £266 10s in 1677–8. Once building work in the Hall was completed in 1680, the throne was installed and embellished with extra carvings by Grinling Gibbons. The room was intended for Garter ceremonies, and Verrio's painted decoration showed Charles himself enthroned in the central oval of the ceiling, and St George and the Dragon above the throne.[23]

Eighteenth-century arrangements remained equally formal, if less elaborate. The description of a new garden building at St James's Palace provided on the occasion of the Prince of Wales's marriage in 1735 does not at first suggest state occasions. It comprised a marble bagnio or bath-house, and a large saloon with pictures and statues on the floor above. Yet it included a red velvet state chair and two stools, embroidered with gold, provided at a cost of £500.[24] Apart from the permanent arrangements at the royal palaces, large numbers of state chairs were required for the great ceremonies of state. At a coronation, for instance, the monarch needed three chairs in the Theatre alone: one for the beginning of the service, the Coronation Chair, and another for the Enthronement (fig.60). More seats

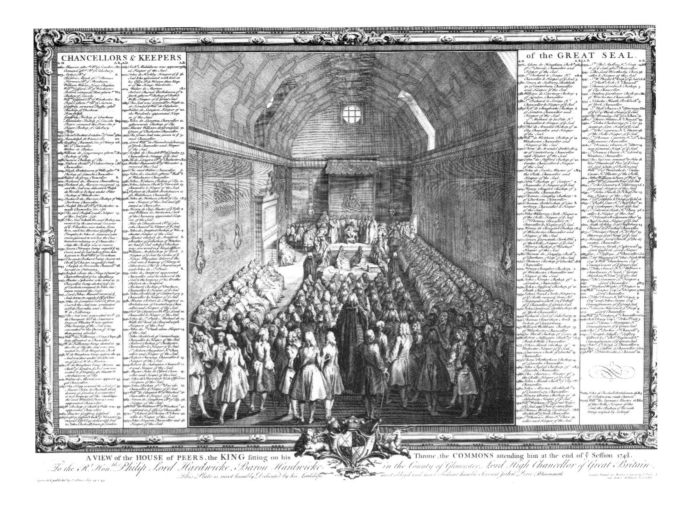

61. View of the House of Lords at the end of the 1741–2 Parliamentary session. George II sits on his throne and the House of Commons is in attendance. Engraving by John Pine, dated 1749. E.813–1959

were needed for the officiating clergy and the monarch's consort, and more again for the preliminary ceremony in Westminster Hall and the banquet afterwards. Tradition also dictated that new thrones should be provided for the first state opening of Parliament of a new reign, both in the House of Lords and the adjoining Prince's Chamber (fig.61). Officials who held state in place of the monarch would also need to be equipped with similar furnishings. When the Earl of Hopton acted as High Commissioner at the Assembly of the Church of Scotland in 1754 in Edinburgh he had two crimson velvet chairs of state. One was placed in the King's Gallery in the church, and another in the Assembly House. The latter was 'entirely new in a very elegant taste' and had a fringed crimson caffoy canopy.[25] Ambassadors were routinely issued with sets of state furniture for the same purpose: surviving mid-eighteenth- and early nineteenth-century 'states' at Knole probably fell into this category.[26]

In these circumstances, it is at first startling to find that only one throne now in the Royal Collection certainly predates the reign of Queen Victoria. It is important to remember that while the Coronation Chair might have become a relic, these thrones were simply furniture. However expensive they were, there was no reason to keep them when they wore out or went out of fashion. Moreover, the survival of the medieval system of perquisites meant court officials like the Lord Great Chamberlain and Lord Chamberlain had a claim on them, especially after the death of a monarch or a coronation. This is why the few remaining eighteenth- and early nineteenth-century royal thrones and stools are mostly to be found in

[25] Public Advertiser, *May 30, 1754.*
[26] *Drury.*

62. View showing state furniture, including the throne in fig.64, set up in the Old State Bedroom at Chatsworth in 1872. Taken from Llewellynn Jewitt, *An illustrated guide to Chatsworth*, Buxton, 1872

country houses like Grimsthorpe and Chatsworth (fig.62),[27] with only chance survivors elsewhere.[28]

Ordering state furniture was a complicated business, since the royal household paid separately for frame and upholstery, seemingly long after this had ceased to be standard practice. There were usually still more bills for the textile used as a top cover, and even the gold lace and embroidery. This reflected an old division between craftsmen of different guilds. The joiner retained the senior position even though the bills put in by the relatively upstart upholsterer would be larger. This was certainly the case with the earliest surviving coronation throne and stool which can be identified with certainty: the examples at Hatfield used by Queen Anne in 1702 (fig.63). The bills show that the frames were provided by Thomas Roberts, who held the warrant of joiner and chair-maker to the royal household between 1685 and 1714, at a cost of £20. The rich blue and gold brocade upholstery was supplied by Anthony Ryland at the much higher cost of £72, and traces of it were still distinguishable when the chair was conserved in the 1960s.[29] The joiner's office was partially hereditary: Richard Roberts, who succeeded Thomas Roberts in 1714, was almost certainly his son. He in turn was followed by Henry Williams and then by Williams' daughter Katherine Naish in 1761. The position included the privilege of wearing livery: when Katherine Naish was sworn in she was granted £8 for a gown of broadcloth and 'Furr of

[27] *These have recently formed the subject of a detailed study (Roberts).*

[28] *For instance the 'King's Chair' at the Treasury, thought to have been made between 1729 and 1742. See W.A. Thorpe, 'Tradition in Treasury furniture II: Walpole and after', Country Life, vol. cix, no. 2817 (12 Jan 1951), pp. 125–8.*

[29] *Anthony Coleridge, 'English furniture and cabinet-makers at Hatfield House', Burlington Magazine, vol. cix, no. 767 (Feb 1967), p. 67.*

63. Chair of state and stool at Hatfield House, used at Queen Anne's coronation in 1702. The gilded frame was supplied by Thomas Roberts, and the chair was originally upholstered by Anthony Ryland in blue and gold brocade

Budge'(lambskin worn with the hairy side facing outwards). The court joiner also provided frames for ambassadorial chairs and stools, like the two sets for the Congress of Brunswick and the Court of France supplied by Richard Roberts in 1720.[30]

As the x-framed chair of state gradually disappeared during the seventeenth century, royal thrones became grander versions of chairs in contemporary domestic use. The Hatfield throne, with its gilded frame and its high back surmounted by the royal arms, sets the pattern for other eighteenth-century examples. Perhaps the most imposing are the thrones and stools supplied for George III and Queen Charlotte's coronation in 1761, now at Chatsworth. Their rococo frames were supplied by Katherine Naish, and upholstered by Vile and Cobb. They still have the original silk brocade covers supplied by Thomas Hinchcliff, though the original gold fringes have now disappeared (fig.64). The same team also supplied two more sets of state furniture for the State Opening of Parliament in the same year: these also survive, though not in their entirety, at Grimsthorpe.

After the long reign of George III, the royal furniture in Parliament was

[30] *Joy 1965, p. 160.*

64. Throne and footstool used by George III at his coronation in 1761. Frames by Katherine Naish, upholstery by Vile and Cobb. Devonshire Collection, Chatsworth House

certainly due for replacement in 1820. Fashions had changed considerably, and such a notable connoisseur of furniture as George IV might be expected to demand something rather special. A promising precedent had been set by two elegant gilt council chairs carved with Greek sphinxes, scrolling acanthus and other neo-classical ornament (fig.65). One is visible in a view of the Throne Room at Carlton House in Pyne's *Royal Residences*, and it seems likely that they were the 'two very large antique elbow chairs' supplied by Tatham and Co. of Mount Street in 1813 for £587 12s 6d. They are certainly taken from designs of antique marble seats published by C. H. Tatham in 1799.[31] However, despite the supervision of Sir John Soane and a bill of well over £3000, the Corinthian canopy and throne supplied for the House of Lords by John Russell, Valance and Evans with upholstery by Elliott and Francis proved rather a disappointment. Surviving views (fig.66) seem to bear out contemporary criticism that while elaborate and costly, the throne was not imposing or dignified and 'fell short of the nursery idea of the King upon his throne'. The throne was evidently dwarfed by the giant canopy, despite being raised on four steps. George IV's coronation was conducted with almost unbelievably lavish pageantry in 1821, five thrones being provided for the abbey alone.

[31] *Exhibition catalogue,* Carlton House: the past glories of George IV's palace, *Queen's Gallery, Buckingham Palace, London, 1991–2, no. 42.*

65. One of two council chairs from Carlton House. Gilded pine and beech. Based on designs by C. H. Tatham and probably supplied by Tatham & Co. in 1813. Royal Collection

66. William IV proroguing Parliament, April 1831. Showing the Soane canopy in the House of Lords. Engraving by H. Melville. E.326–1942

67. Footstool made for the Coronation Chair for George IV's coronation in 1821, by Bailey and Saunders. Beechwood, carved and gilt: the silk velvet upholstery is a later replacement. On loan to the Undercroft Museum, Westminster Abbey. W.7–1991

68. State throne supplied for Buckingham Palace by Dowbiggin in 1837. Royal Collection

69. The throne end of the House of Lords, designed by Charles Barry and A.W.N. Pugin, in 1849. From H.T. Ryde, *Illustrations of the New Palace of Westminster*, 1849

Even the Coronation Chair was completely upholstered in 'Gold Frosted Tabby', and provided with a new footstool (fig.67).[32] Russell, Vallance and Evans once more supplied most of the furniture. Bailey and Saunders did most of the upholstery, and their bill alone came to over £5000. This proved to be the last full coronation on the medieval model. Appalled by the memory of its extravagance,[33] William IV at first wished to dispense with the service altogether, but eventually compromised by spending as little as possible on the 1831 'Penny Coronation'. The procession, banquet and other ceremonies in Westminster Hall were scrapped, and the Duke of Devonshire had great difficulty in establishing his claim to the old thrones used in the Abbey after the event. The same mood of austerity characterised Queen Victoria's coronation in 1838. New pieces were of course still occasionally needed, like the State Throne in the Throne Room at Buckingham Palace supplied by Dowbiggin of Mount Street in 1837 (fig.68). Stylistically, it is not very different to some of George IV's thrones, but it was much cheaper: only £1187 for throne and canopy.[34]

The new throne provided in the House of Lords some ten years later marks an important change of direction. When the Palace of Westminster was rebuilt after the fire of 1834, the perquisites system was at last falling into disuse. The Gothic canopy and throne has therefore remained almost exactly as Charles Barry and A.W.N. Pugin designed it (fig.69). The story

[32] *See Christopher Wilk, 'Recent acquisitions of furniture and woodwork at the Victoria and Albert Museum', Burlington Magazine, vol. cxxxv, no. 1083 (June 1993), pp. 444–5.*

[33] *Cf. Geoffrey de Bellaigue, 'A Royal mise-en-scène: George IV's coronation banquet', Furniture History, vol. XXIX (1993), pp. 174–83 for an authoritative and entertaining description.*

[34] *Smith, p. 147.*

70. Chair for Prince Albert's use in the House of Lords, made by John Webb of Bond Street in 1847. Gilded wood, upholstered in velvet. Loaned to the V&A by the Trustees of the National Heritage Memorial Fund

behind the choice of the Gothic style for the architecture of the new Palace of Westminster, historic seat of the mother of parliaments and of constitutional government, is well known.[35] It indicates a new feeling that the styles of the past could and should be resurrected to lend their dignity and authority to commissions of this kind. This has remained a lasting influence on the design of thrones and chairs of state: it was of course part of a much wider nineteenth-century revival of interest in historic styles which affected every aspect of the decorative arts. The Westminster throne and the x-framed chairs for the heir and consort (fig.70) were supplied in 1847, by craftsmen who worked regularly with Pugin and shared his preoccupations. The maker, John Webb of Old Bond Street, was also well-known as a dealer in antiquities and paintings,[36] while the gilded enamels set into the throne were supplied by Hardman & Co. of Birmingham.[37] Through the design of the throne and especially through its rigorously architectural setting, Barry and Pugin skilfully managed to suggest both the dignity and pre-eminence of the Crown, and its separation from everyday politics. It is of course still used every autumn for its intended purpose at the state opening of Parliament, when the Lords and the Commons assemble in this chamber to hear the Queen's Speech. Newspaper and television coverage of this event has ensured that it has become one of our most enduring and familiar images of royalty.

[35] See, for instance, M.H. Port, The Houses of Parliament, New Haven and London, Paul Mellon Centre/Yale University Press, 1976.

[36] Wainwright, pp. 45–6.

[37] Wedgwood and House of Lords, A report by the Victoria and Albert Museum concerning the furniture in the House of Lords, London, HMSO, 1974, p. 12.

CHAPTER IV
OFFICIAL BODIES AND SOCIETIES

Many kinds of officials use throne-like seats besides royalty and the clergy. Amongst them are those presiding over the deliberations of courts of justice, civic corporations, livery companies and learned societies, as well as sociable bodies like masonic lodges and dining clubs. Their chairs form the largest group to be considered here, and a surprising number of post-medieval examples survive. Most are enlarged, high-backed versions of contemporary domestic armchairs. They may be raised up on a platform, and will usually be decorated with the institution's coat of arms, or other appropriate emblems. There may be other distinctive seats nearby for lesser officials. The distinctions between chairs made for different kinds of institutions usually arise in their decorative detailing, rather than their form or usage. It therefore seems most appropriate to consider them all together, in a roughly chronological sequence.

CHAIR.

From St Mary's Hall, Coventry

71. Master's chair of the United Guild of Coventry, in St Mary's Hall, Coventry. Oak, about 1450–60. The decoration includes a figure of St Mary, and finials in the form of royal lions and the elephant and castle of Coventry. From Henry Shaw, *Specimens of Ancient Furniture*, London, 1836

72. The Deacon Convener's Chair of the
Aberdeen Incorporated Trades, presented by
Matthew Guild in about 1570. Oak, about
1560–70, incorporating earlier tracery work.
Trinity Hall, Aberdeen

73. Wrights' and Coopers' Chair, given by
Jerome Blak. Oak, dated 1574. Trinity Hall,
Aberdeen

Before 1700

Surviving examples of medieval ceremonial seating are usually associated
with royalty or the clergy, but it has already become apparent that they
were not exclusively reserved for their use. A chancellor, ambassador or
other official representing the monarch did so in quasi-regal state. In the
hierarchical society of the middle ages, the best seat was automatically
allotted to the most authoritative person present, even in the home. This
would not necessarily have meant anything very grand, but it seems
likely that the more wealthy and powerful medieval guilds and livery
companies, for instance, would have commissioned special seating for
their splendid halls. An early guild throne survives at St Mary's Hall,
Coventry, which was built in 1340–2 and enlarged in about 1400. The

74. Fleshers' Chair, given by Andrew Watson. Mahogany, dated 1661. Trinity Hall, Aberdeen

Gothic throne (fig.71) probably dates from 1450–60. The triple back may refer to the united guilds of St Mary, St John and St Catherine. It has been suggested this was a double seat, for joint use by the Master and the Mayor, but ceremonial seats are usually generously scaled in any case.[1]

An even more remarkable survival is the group of twenty chairs at Trinity Hall, the headquarters of the Aberdeen Incorporated Trades. These were presented to the association between the mid-sixteenth and eighteenth centuries by members of the constituent craft guilds, usually to mark their term of office as deacon. Before the first Hall was built in 1633, meetings were held in the Deacon Convener's house. The earliest chair, presented in about 1570, is reserved for his use (fig.72). It is said to incorporate parts of the choir stalls of the 'Mither Kirk', carved in about 1507 by John Fendour. The donor had apparently been

[1] *Joan Cadogan Lancaster,* Guide to St Mary's Hall, *Coventry, City of Coventry, 1948, pp. 26, 45.*

75. Tailors' Chair, given by Thomas Gardine. Oak, dated 1627. Trinity Hall, Aberdeen

involved in their removal in 1560, at the time of the Reformation. The first firmly dated example is a solid joined armchair (fig.73), and a more elaborate mahogany example given in 1661 (fig.74) may be compared to a chair made from the timbers of the *Golden Hind* around the same date (fig.113). The Tailors' Chair of 1627 (fig.75) may represent most of the others. It is oak, with a tall narrow back. This is carved with the name or initials of the donor, the date of his gift, and other appropriate emblems, in this case his arms and a pair of scissors. The arms curve round with the seat, which broadens considerably from back to front.[2]

The Tailors' chair and its companions are essentially grander versions of common domestic types, rendered more imposing by extended backs and appropriate decoration. The same features characterise other ceremonial chairs of the period, like two chairs from the Salisbury Council House

[2] *Learmont.*

which were made to the same pattern nearly forty years apart (fig.76). The second has been attributed to Humphrey Beckham of Salisbury (1588–1671), who served as Chamberlain and Warden to the local joiners' company.[3] Fig.77 is one of a group of four armchairs of around 1600 from the north-west of England, all with rectangular seats and arcaded backs and none of them unfortunately in original condition. Their elaborate decoration suggests some kind of ceremonial use, though their purpose has not been established.[4] The Warburton chair (fig.78) is more sophisticated, incorporating a marquetry panel of a type often associated with immigrant German craftsmen. At one point it was in Horace Walpole's collection at Strawberry Hill.[5]

In marked contrast is the Speaker's Chair made for the House of Commons in 1645–6 (fig.79). Although it is freestanding, its form derives from architecture rather than domestic furniture. The Renaissance had finally arrived: the principles of classical architecture had been thoroughly absorbed, not just plundered for decorative motifs. It can be compared to later examples of built-in seating, for instance at St Paul's (figs.20,21), or the Earl Marshal's Court at the College of Arms, fitted out soon after 1707

76. Two walnut chairs made for the Salisbury Council House, bearing the arms of the Corporation of New Sarum. The chair on the right is dated 1585 and was given by Mayor Robert Bower, whose initials it bears. The other is dated 1622, with the initials of the donor, the mayor Maurice Green, and is attributed to the joiner Humphrey Beckham of Salisbury. Salisbury and South Wiltshire Museum

[3] *Chinnery, pp. 448–54 & 550–3.*
[4] *Christopher Gilbert,* Furniture at Temple Newsam and Lotherton Hall, *London, National Art-Collections Fund and Leeds Art Collections Fund, 1978, vol. i, no. 47.*
[5] *It was included in the 1842 sale (lot 117) and was purchased by the Earl of Derby, according to Margaret Jourdain,* English Decoration and Furniture of the Early Renaissance, *London, Batsford, fig. 354.*

77. Chair from Hornby Castle, Yorkshire. Cedar and oak, about 1600: the feet, stretchers and lower cross-rail renewed. The arms are those of a hereditary Keepership or Wardenship connected with the castle's owners. Temple Newsam House (Leeds City Art Galleries)

6 *W.H. Godfrey,* The College of Arms, *London, London Survey Committee, 1960, p. 20.*

(fig.80).[6] The new Speaker's Chair was the most important of a series of improvements to the House of Commons carried out by the Office of Works during the Civil War period. As a symbol of the Speaker's authority it was, after all, an object of considerable ceremonial significance. The incident of the Five Members had demonstrated this even before war broke out. Charles I entered the House of Commons on 4 January 1642, hoping to arrest John Pym and four other MPs accused of treason. He asked to borrow the Speaker's Chair since traditionally the Speaker was the Crown's representative in the House. The Speaker, William Lenthall, surrendered his chair but when Charles asked him whether the five members were present, he fell to his knees and announced that it was not his part either to speak or see but as the House desired, 'whose servant I am here'. In fact the birds had already flown and Charles left in 'a more discontented and angry passion than he came in'. The new seat was upholstered in velvet, and carved with four Corinthian capitals, two scrolls and a frontispiece, and the king's arms and supporters 'to be seene on both sides'. The carver, Zachary Taylor, was also employed by the Office of Works at St Paul's, Covent Garden. The king's execution was still several

78. Chair made for Sir Peter Warburton (1540?–1621), Justice of the Common Pleas, of Grafton Hall, Cheshire. Walnut, with a marquetry panel in the back bearing his arms and dated 1603. Private collection

79. The Speaker's Chair in the House of Commons. 1645–6, with velvet upholstery and carved decoration by Zachary Taylor. From a sketch by Sir James Thornhill (1675–1734) in the Greater London Record Office

years away: the Royal Arms would be removed during the Commonwealth period and replaced in February 1663. The seat itself seems to have survived until the 1834 fire, with some alterations. Eighteenth- and nineteenth-century illustrations show the Speaker sitting in front of what looks like the same structure in a more conventional chair (fig.81). This chair had to be renewed regularly, being treated by retiring Speakers as a perquisite of office in a way which became familiar in the last chapter. A wooden canopy with linenfold and flamboyant panelling in Radley Church, Berkshire, may have been associated with the pre-Civil War Speaker's Chair, and is presumed to have been acquired by Lenthall in the same way.[7]

7 *Sir Bryan H. Fell and K.R. Mackenzie,* The Houses of Parliament: a guide to the Palace of Westminster, *London, HMSO, 1988.*

The eighteenth and early nineteenth centuries

Most of the halls belonging to the City of London livery companies had to be rebuilt after the Great Fire of 1666. Despite war damage and redevelopment, around a hundred companies and some forty-three halls still exist today. Sets of matched chairs were usually provided for Court Rooms, and sometimes other rooms as well. These often included larger chairs for the Master or other presiding official, and perhaps his assistants. No pre-Fire examples survive, although they evidently existed: the Drapers in 1569–70 for instance paid over £10 for a walnut chair with four crimson velvet cushions for the Warden.[8] The surviving examples are mostly eighteenth or nineteenth century: many were included in the V&A's exhibition of livery company treasures held in 1926. The series of record photos taken for this is especially valuable, since some of the chairs were subsequently destroyed in the Blitz.[9] Amongst them was one of the earliest examples, the caned chair belonging to the Parish Clerks' Company (fig.82). This is known to have been presented in 1716, though stylistically it could have been made twenty years earlier.[10]

Perhaps the Parish Clerks' chair was made to match an existing chair, like the Salisbury chairs. Companies also copied each other's chairs. The Dyers' Company commissioned a new Prime Warden's Chair in 1734, as

80. The Hall of the Heralds' College, with an imaginary reconstruction of the Earl Marshal's Court. Aquatint after Pugin and Rowlandson in Rudolph Ackermann, *Microcosm of London*, London, 1811

[8] *Revd. A.H. Jonson,* A History of the Worshipful Company of Drapers, *Oxford, Clarendon Press, 1915, vol. ii, p. 223.*

[9] Livery Companies: V&A *and* Livery Companies: Country Life. *Further photographs are filed under the names of the lenders in the Museum's Picture Library.*

[10] *R.H. Adams,* The Parish Clerks of London, *London & Chichester, Phillimore, 1971.*

81. The House of Commons. Aquatint after Pugin and Rowlandson in Rudolph Ackermann, *Microcosm of London*, London, 1811

part of a programme of repairs and refurbishment of the Court Room (fig.83). On 8 January 1734 the Company agreed with Abraham Saunders of Cateaton Street for 24 chairs with close nailed upholstery 'to be done in a very handsome and substantial manner' for ten shillings apiece, and a 'Master's Chair to be done with blue morocco Leather to be Naild with handsome lacquered Nails and a handsome Wallnut Tree frame resembling the pattern of the Master's chair of the Skinners Company' for the sum of £5. On 5 February it was further agreed that Saunders should add the company's arms to the top of the chair for another guinea, and that the cover should be of 'Red Turkey Leather'.[11] This is the first piece of furniture attributable to this maker, who is perhaps the Saunders of Cateaton Street recorded in 1749 and the Abraham Saunders at the same address in 1762.[12] The Skinners were and are the Dyers' neighbours on Dowgate Hill, but unfortunately their model chair no longer exists and is not mentioned in their records. Stylistically, it cannot have been made long before: it may be significant that the Dyers had stored the Skinners' furniture in their hall in 1732.[13] The close links within City communities probably generated a good deal of repeat business within the same circle of craftsmen. Edward Newman, who made the Gothick Master's Chair of the Joiners' Company in 1754 (fig.84), may also have been the 'Mr Newman' responsible for providing the Vintners' Company with new tables and other furnishings for the

[11] *John Norman Daynes,* A short history of the Ancient Mistery of the Dyers of the City of London, *London, published by the company, 1965, p. 36, and the Court Minute Book of the Company in Guildhall Library.*

[12] Dictionary, *p. 782.*

[13] *Information from the Skinners' records kindly supplied by their Beadle, Mr E.J. Hall.*

82. Master's Chair of the Parish Clerks' Company. Walnut with caned upholstery, carved with the company's arms and chants from the psalms. Given by Samuel Andrews in 1716

83. The Prime Warden's Chair of the Dyers Company. Walnut with leather upholstery, supplied by Abraham Saunders of Cateaton Street in 1734

Court Room in 1742–3. The fullbloodedly rococo master's chair, appropriately garnished with a mask of Bacchus and bunches of grapes, was presumably part of this commission (fig.85).[14] In some cases the company's arms seem to have been separately supplied by a specialised heraldic carver. The Minute Book of the Glaziers Company, for instance, recorded on 7 November 1768 that a past master, Lake Young, had presented 'a very ellegant Chair for the Master of the Company for the time being to sit in with the Arms of the Company carved and affixed on the Top of the Back'.[15] This would also account for the rather topheavy appearance of the Watermen and Lightermen's chair of 1800, with its magnificently carved and gilded Royal Arms (fig.86).

Ceremonial chairs commissioned by other kinds of societies also begin to appear in quantity in the eighteenth century. Attempts to identify these in contemporary records can be frustrating. The continuing amalgamations and alterations of masonic lodges, for instance, means that even where early chairs are still in their original homes, records of their commission

[14] *Minutes of the Court of Assistants of the Vintners' Company, Guildhall Library, 1741–3.*

[15] *Charles Henry Ashdown,* History of the Worshipful Company of Glaziers, *London, privately printed, 1919, p. 84.*

84. Master's Chair of the Joiners' Company, on loan to the Victoria and Albert Museum. Mahogany, carved in 1754 for £27 6s 0d by Edward Newman (Master in 1749)

have often gone astray. There has also always been a lively trade in secondhand masonic regalia. As early as 1744 a notice of a sale at Mansion House in the City of London draws attention to 'an extraordinary good Free-Mason's Chair, with a set of Mahogany Square Tables, with Bolts that confine them together, being as good as new'.[16] An early illustration of English Freemasons (fig.87) includes an L-shaped table which could have been made up from tables of this kind: the ritual shown is probably a preparation for Labour.[17] To the left is the Master's throne, apparently a wide upholstered armchair of the kind sometimes called a 'love seat'. Its extended back panel is pierced and carved with masonic emblems. Each of these has a symbolic meaning: the sun and moon and globe represent enlightenment, while the square and compasses are united to regulate lives and actions. The accumulation of these emblems makes masonic chairs easy to recognise, though it should be remembered that some symbols, such as the sun and moon or the compasses, have a long history and may

[16] Daily Advertiser, *Thursday 29 November, 1744.*

[17] *Erich Lindner,* Die Königliche Kunst im Bild, *Graz, Akademische Druck, 1976, pp. 256–7.*

85. Master's Chair of the Vintners' Company. Mahogany, probably supplied in 1742–3 by Edward Newman

be found elsewhere (fig.24). There are two more high-backed chairs with cabriole legs for the Senior and Junior Wardens. Other masons sit on ordinary ladderback chairs, of a kind one might expect to find in the taverns and coffee houses where lodges commonly met at this date. Some are listed in the table of lodges in the background, which is surmounted by the arms of Lord Weymouth, the Grand Master. This was compiled from a list of lodges published in 1735 by the engraver John Pine (1690–1756). Pine specialised in heraldic and ceremonial work, a connection fostered by his appointment as Bluemantle Pursuivant in 1743: one of his engravings is reproduced elsewhere (fig.61). Picard notes that the lodges are arranged in order of foundation (the earliest dating from 1691) and comments on the social diversity of their membership.

More surprising is the chair made for the President of the Society of Dilettanti in 1739 by Elka Haddock (fig.88). This was described as a 'mahogany compass elboe seat' and was supplied with a mahogany pedestal on castors, at a cost of £4 10s 0d. It was originally covered in 4 3/8 yards

86. Master's Chair of the Watermen and Lightermen's Company. Gilded wood with leather upholstery, presented by the company's rulers in 1800

of the 'richest Genoa velvet' in crimson, purchased from John Atkinson for £5 13s 9d. The maker is also recorded as supplying furniture for Wilton, Rousham and Moulton Hall in Essex. It is of course a laterally-oriented x-framed chair, and in this most unusual case the form was evidently a self-consciously archaic choice, of a kind which would become more familiar in the next century. The society's interests centred around the convivial study of classical archaeology, and the President's Chair was known as the 'sella curulis'. Two years later the society decided the President should assume 'Roman dress', in the form of a scarlet toga, whenever he used it. This seems to have created some initial embarrassment or discomfort: in 1741 President Gray had to be reprimanded for his 'high Misdemeanour. . . . in neglecting the Insignia of the Office'. However, the tradition stuck and soon other officials were put into fancy dress too.[18]

The President's Chair made in 1759–60 for the Society of Arts to the design of Sir William Chambers is more conventional, but still unlike most domestic furniture of the same date (fig.89). Its seat rail and legs are of a straightness and squareness otherwise unknown in this country until

[18] *Cecil Harcourt Smith*, The Society of Dilettanti, its regalia and pictures, together with an outline of its history, *London, Macmillan, 1932, pp. 32–4 & Lionel Cust*, History of the Society of Dilettanti, *London, Macmillan, 1927, pp. 25–7.*

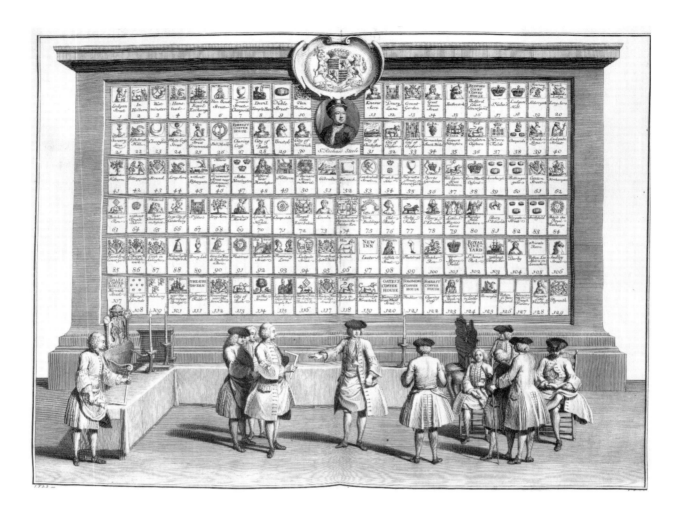

the late 1760s, which has led to it being described as 'the earliest neo-classic chair in England'.[19] It is the only surviving element of the furnishings designed by Chambers for the Great Room in the Society's new premises in Little Denmark Court off the Strand. It was made in mahogany and upholstered in green velvet, with an outer protective cover, for £17 8s 6d, probably by Charles Ross who provided the tables and benches for the Great Room. It may be compared to a chair design in an album which Chambers compiled from all the small drawings he made in France and Italy between 1749 and 1755 (fig.90). Such a design would have been very advanced anywhere at that date: it is interesting to note that its back is more 'correctly' neo-classical than the Society of Arts chair.

This again raises a stylistic question connected with seats of authority. Why do dated examples of masters' chairs sometimes look rather old-fashioned? This seems to have been largely accidental. Setting aside a special case like the Dilettanti's *sella curulis* (which in any case seems to have been intended as something of a joke), there is little evidence to suggest that historic styles were deliberately used to convey authority before the nineteenth century. Furniture in the height of fashion was the exception rather than the rule, being made for a relatively restricted clientele by a small number of makers, almost exclusively based in the West End. From the second half of the eighteenth century printed designs

87. English Freemasons, engraved by I.F. after I.F.D.B., in Bernard Picard, *Cérémonies et coutumes religieuses de tous les peuples du monde*, Amsterdam, 1736

[19] *Harris.*

88. The *sella curulis* of the Society of Dilettanti. Mahogany with velvet upholstery, supplied by Elka Haddock in 1739

[20] *A set of masonic chairs made by a firm in Wakefield, Yorkshire, for the local masonic hall in 1768 still incorporate rococo carving, for instance. See Christopher Gilbert, 'Wright and Elwick of Wakefield, 1748–1824: a study of provincial patronage', Furniture History, vol. xii (1976), pp. 35–50.*

[21] *Peter Ward-Jackson,* English Furniture Designs of the Eighteenth Century, *London, HMSO, 1958.*

[22] *Ernest Arthur Ebblewhite,* The history of the Shakespear Lodge no. 99, 1757–1904, *London (privately printed), 1905, pp. 47–8 and* The property of the Shakespear Lodge, *London (privately printed), 1936, pp. 10–12.*

circulated outside London, but new ideas were not necessarily adopted very quickly.[20] In any case, the relatively small demand meant there were few printed designs specifically for ceremonial chairs. Those that did appear might already be outmoded. George Hepplewhite included designs for state chairs in the first edition of his *Cabinet-Maker and Upholsterer's Guide* (1788)(fig.91), but these were amongst the designs criticised by Thomas Sheraton in his *Cabinet-Maker and Upholsterer's Drawing Book* (1791) as having 'already caught the decline', and were accordingly withdrawn from the 1794 edition.[21] Most clients and makers seem to have been unaware of, or at least untroubled by, the situation. Many pieces were selected by committee, a procedure which rarely leads to adventurous decisions. Nevertheless, there are surviving examples which show it was always possible to achieve something more up-to-date, either by going straight to a good West End firm, or by taking a good deal of personal trouble.

When the Shakespear Lodge of London needed new master's and wardens' chairs in 1779, for instance, they set aside £21. The treasurer obtained a first design which was rejected as unsuitable, and a committee was set up to deal with the project. After experiencing further difficulties and wasting thirty shillings, it eventually managed to obtain an 'excellent design' gratis from one of the lodge's own members. Another member charged £20 18s 0d to make up the chairs, which still survive (fig.92).[22]

89. The President's Chair of the Society of Arts. Mahogany with velvet upholstery, supplied in 1759–60 to the design of Sir William Chambers. Royal Society of Arts

They represent a sophisticated but individual interpretation of current neo-classical taste, almost mannerist in their elongated forms, and the quality of the workmanship is also high. All three are the same size and there is no lavish display of symbolic ornament, but the appropriate architectural order has been discreetly used on each chair to make its purpose clear.[23] The designer was John Yenn (1750–1821), a pupil and assistant of William Chambers who held various posts in the Office of Works: he succeeded Chambers as Treasurer at the Royal Academy, incurring the dislike of Benjamin West who thought his 'watery eye' was a sure sign of a treacherous character. He is now probably best remembered for his high-quality coloured architectural drawings and designs.[24] The maker was William Fleming, a Chandos Street cabinet-maker and upholsterer; these are the first surviving pieces to be attributed to him.[25]

[23] *The Ionic order on the Master's chair signifies wisdom, with Doric for strength on the Senior Warden's, and Corinthian for beauty on the Junior Warden's. This is the standard modern arrangement, though Joy notes that it was not always followed in the eighteenth century.*

[24] *Colvin, p. 964.*

[25] Dictionary, p. 304.

90. Design for a chair by Sir William Chambers, about 1755

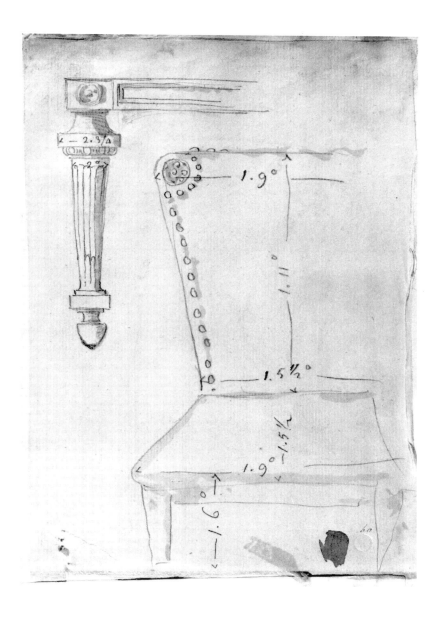

The leading Freemasons at Grand Lodge were prepared to go to considerable expense in 1791, to find furnishings befitting 'the high honour the Society now enjoys of his Royal Highness the Prince of Wales being Grand Master'.[26] On 18 February the Hall Committee declared that they were 'open to receive Designs and Estimates' for a Grand Master's Throne and two Grand Wardens' Chairs, and for candlesticks. Unfortunately, details of the unsuccessful applicants and their designs do not survive. If a surviving sheet of designs by George Speer of Great Tower Street was amongst them, as seems likely, it would certainly have made a dowdy contrast to the chairs created by the winner, Robert Kennett, in the fashionable French taste (fig.93).[27] Kennett attended a meeting where the committee selected a pattern of Garter blue velvet and instructed him about masonic ornament. He must then have worked very speedily, putting the chairs on display at his Bond Street showroom by the end of April. He was evidently an astute self-publicist, arranging for a series of puffs in the *Oracle* which invited the public to come and join the 'great

[26] *Algernon Tudor-Craig*, Catalogue of the contents of the Museum of Freemasons' Hall, *London, United Grand Lodge, 1938, Joy, and Hewitt.*

[27] *Anthony Coleridge, 'George Speer: A Newly Identified Georgian Cabinet-maker',* Apollo, *vol. xcii (1970), pp. 274–83.*

91. Design for state chairs dated 1787. George Hepplewhite, *The Cabinet-Maker and Upholsterer's Guide*, 1788

92. Master's, Senior and Junior Wardens' chairs of the Shakespear Lodge, London. Gilded mahogany, cedar and lime with gilt-brass columns in the back and velvet upholstery. Designed by John Yenn and made by William Fleming in 1779

93. Grand Master's and Wardens' Chairs. Made for the Grand Lodge of England in 1791 by Robert Kennett, for the use of the Prince of Wales. Carved and gilded wood with blue velvet upholstery. Freemasons' Hall

number of the Nobility . . . who have exceedingly flattered Mr Kennett, by assuring him, that they are by far the most beautiful of the kind ever seen, both in point of design and execution. . .'.[28] He was briefly a favourite with members of the Anglo-Irish aristocracy, but went out of business after 1795 and was reduced to curing toothache by 1804: later still he disappeared altogether in his attempts to evade his creditors.[29] On this occasion his bill came to £210 2s 0d: parts of this were disallowed but the eventual cost of £165 10s 0d was still higher than the Committee's original estimates of £100–130. The upholstery of the Grand Master's throne was originally much more elaborate, the back being embroidered with a masonic symbol and draped with swags of material and a garland of artificial flowers. This can be glimpsed in contemporary portraits of the Prince of Wales and his Acting Grand Master, the Earl of Moira, but is most clearly seen in an 1833 portrait of the Duke of Sussex (fig.94). The chair was probably reupholstered for the Prince of Wales's installation in 1875; the surmounting coronet and feathers were replaced by a coronet and cushion in 1901, when the Duke of Connaught became Grand Master.

A few chairs of this kind were designed by well-known architects, like Sir John Soane and Charles Heathcot Tatham who have already appeared in the last chapter. Soane was a Freemason, and designed a new hall for Grand Lodge in 1828.[30] He contributed £500 towards the building, which was completed by 1831 but no longer survives. He and Gandy supplied detailed views of alternative treatments for the interior which include two thrones (fig.95 and cover). One is supported by lions, but

[28] The Oracle, 28 April, 30 April, 2 May 1791: references in the Library at Freemasons' Hall supplied by Mrs C.E. Lloyd-Jacob.

[29] Dictionary, pp. 506–7.

[30] Pierre de la Ruffinière du Prey, Sir John Soane, London, Victoria and Albert Museum, 1985, pp. 83–4, 112.

94. Portrait of HRH Augustus Frederick, Duke of Sussex, Grand Master 1813–43. Lithograph of 1833 by John Harris, showing the original upholstery of the Grand Master's Throne. Freemasons' Hall

95. Sir John Soane. Design for a new Masonic Hall in Great Queen Street, 1828. Pencil, pen and sepia ink with brown, red, green blue and yellow wash. 3307.201

96. 'No. 1. A design for the throne of Week's Mechanical Museum', signed by Charles Heathcot Tatham and dated 1798. E.400–1929

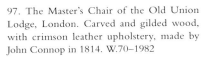

97. The Master's Chair of the Old Union Lodge, London. Carved and gilded wood, with crimson leather upholstery, made by John Connop in 1814. W.70–1982

98. Chair of office dated 1750, probably made for a mock corporation. Oak with walnut veneer and painted decoration. On loan to the Grosvenor Museum, Chester

they are rather conventional-looking pieces of furniture which do not seem to fit this eerie interior especially well. They may have been existing objects rather than his own design, though no trace of them survives today. It is not clear whether the Tatham design produced in 1798 (fig.96) was ever used. The perfumer and machinist Thomas Weeks had leased a large exhibition room in Tichborne Street, Westminster in 1797. The first reference to his mechanical museum, in 1802, states that 'this Museum . . . when complete, will form an interesting object to the curious. The grand room, which is 107 feet long, and 30 feet high, is covered entirely with blue satin, and contains a variety of figures, which exhibit the effects of mechanism in an astonishing manner. The architecture is by Wyatt; the painting on the ceiling is by Rebecca and Singleton.' The star attractions included mechanical models of a bird of paradise and a steel tarantula which 'darts out by itself from a box . . . and, in fact, performs all the appropriate movements of the insect which it represents'.[31] Unless Weeks hoped for a royal opening, Tatham's throne

[31] F.H.W. Sheppard (ed.), The Survey of London, London, Athlone Press, vol. xxxi (1968: St James Westminster II), pp. 54–6.

99. The Mayor's Seat in the Mayor's Parlour of the Honourable Incorporation of the King's Arms Kitchen, Chester. Oak, carved with wheat sheaves, roses, thistles and shamrocks and the motto of the City of Chester; brown leather upholstery. About 1850. On loan to the Grosvenor Museum, Chester

can only have been intended as a kind of theatrical prop in such a setting. The portrait framed by a garter star and draperies beneath the royal arms is presumably George III, and the small grotto-fountains surmounted by Neptune's trident on either side could no doubt have been mechanically operated. The throne itself is a low bench raised on a stepped platform and flanked by candelabra: an ingenious design which would have provided an architectural focus for the Great Room without taking up much of its floorspace.

There were fashions in symbolism as well as style. The crocodile motif on the back of a masonic chair made for the Old Union Lodge of London in 1814 (fig.97), like the carved wooden fringing which decorates its seat rail, may be paralleled on fashionable domestic furniture of the same date. The 'Egyptomania' of the early nineteenth century was stimulated by archaeological publications and events like Nelson's victory at the Battle of the Nile in 1798, and had infected almost every aspect of the decorative arts. Amongst its victims were the Freemasons, who were moved to claim ancient Egypt as one of their spiritual homes: at least two Egyptian-style masonic halls were built around this time, in Edinburgh

100. Oak armchair, dated 1585, at the Society of Antiquaries of London. This was the High President's Chair of the Noviomagians Society, founded in 1828

101. The Master's Chair of the Broderers' Company. Oak with leather upholstery: partly seventeenth century but extensively restored by George Sayffort or Scyffert in 1836. The chair was destroyed in 1941

and Boston.[32] In this instance, as the lodge history explains, the crocodile represents the Deity, since according to Plutarch the creature has a thin transparent membrane over its eyes 'by reason of which it sees and is not seen, as God sees all, Himself not being seen'. The chair was made by a member of the lodge, the carver and gilder John Connop of St Ann's Lane, Aldersgate: he charged his brethren £20 for the chair and they were 'much pleased with the elegance of the same'. His trade card survives in the Banks Collection in the British Museum. Interestingly, like some others it includes an inconspicuous masonic symbol (the square and compasses), probably in an attempt to build up business connections generally rather than specifically to obtain more such commissions.[33] Although lodge furniture was often made by members, this could not by itself have been a very lucrative source of trade. Again, we may note that when new Senior and Junior Wardens' chairs were presented to the Lodge in 1833, the same pattern − now nearly twenty years old − was used, minus the crocodile.

There were many drinking and dining clubs in the eighteenth century besides the Freemasons. They catered for different levels of society but

[32] *James Stevens-Curl, 'Legends of the Craft: the Architecture of Masonic Halls',* Country Life, *vol. clxxx, no. 4644 (21 August 1986), pp. 581–3.*

[33] *Graham 1988, and Sir Gerald W. Wollaston & J. Tindall-Robertson, A Short History of the Old Union Lodge, 1935.*

102. The dining room of the Sublime Society of Beefsteaks at the Lyceum, furnished in about 1838. From a sketch by James Hallett illustrated in Walter Arnold, *The Life and Death of the Sublime Society of Beefsteaks*, London, 1871

34 *One dated 1741 and belonging to the Duke of Westminster was included in an exhibition of* The Grosvenor Treasures, *Eaton Hall, Chester, 1984, cat. 56.*

35 *P.J. Boughton (ed),* The Clowes Family of Chester Sporting Artists *(exhibition catalogue), Grosvenor Museum, Chester, 1985, pp. 16–17.*

were invariably masculine in their membership. Ceremonial was evidently one of the attractions, and a distinctive seat was often provided for the master (fig.3). Some societies took the form of mock corporations, and elected a mayor and other officials. The one at Sefton mentioned in chapter II even had its own church pew. A chair on loan to the Grosvenor Museum in Chester was presumably made for such a society (fig.98). One inscription refers to 'Tho: Cholmondeley of Vale Royal Esq. Mayor/Anno Domini 1750', but the other inscription and the head of Silenus impart a more Bacchic note. Other chairs of the same type exist.[34] The Grosvenor Museum also holds the entire furnishings of the Mayor's Parlour of the Honourable Incorporation of the King's Arms Kitchen, another mock corporation based in a Chester pub whose records go back to 1770. In 1821 they decided to improve their premises by acquiring a sword of state and a mace, as well as asking 'Mr Alderman Hodkinson' to make a suitable seat for the Mayor: this was surmounted by a panel painted with the Royal Arms by the local painter Daniel Clowes.[35] The present seat looks like a replacement, perhaps made some thirty years later (fig.99).

103. Bardic chair presented to the victor of the National Eisteddfod of Wales in 1887. Dantzic oak: designed by Morris Henry Roberts of the firm of Austin and M.H.Roberts, Llangollen. Illustrated in *The Cabinet Maker and Art Furnisher*, 1 September 1887

Antiquarianism and the Victorians

The nineteenth-century fashion for old oak and other antiquarian furnishings was ideally suited to this clubby masculine atmosphere. An oak chair dated 1585 found an especially appropriate use as the High President's Chair of the Noviomagians, a dining club founded as an offshoot of the Society of Antiquaries in 1828 (fig.100).[36] Contacts amongst the Noviomagians would be the source of many of the chairs in George Godwin's collection, discussed in Chapter V. Meanwhile, Mr John Beauchamp of the Broderers' Company discovered in 1836 'an ancient chair which he had no doubt had formerly been used as the seat of the Master'(fig.101). Although it was very mutilated and decayed he had it

[36] *T.D. Kendrick and H. Clifford Smith, 'The Chair of the Noviomagians', The Antiquaries Journal, vol. xxvii–iii (1947–8), pp. 183–5.*

104. The Tarporley Hunt Chair, dated 1862. One of a group of photographs of carvings in wood by William Gibbs Rogers (1792–1875) purchased by the Victoria and Albert Museum in 1877 from R. Jackson

restored 'as nearly as he could judge, to its original state' to serve its original purpose for the sum of £10 7s 0d by 'Geo. Sayffort'. This may be the George Scyffert recorded at 81 Margaret Street, Cavendish Square, in 1820.[37] The author of the company history jocularly comments 'there is one peculiarity in this chair which lays it open to the censorious to imagine that in former days sobriety was not conspicuous by its absence [*sic*], for the right arm of the Chair has a hinge which enables it to be raised, so that the occupant would find no difficulty in vacating his position, either by his own free-will or by the help of the attendants'.[38] Insobriety and practical jokes frequently characterised the proceedings of another dining club, the Sublime Society of Beefsteaks, which had been founded in 1735. This moved into a new purpose-built suite of rooms in the Lyceum Theatre in 1838, where it remained until it closed down and its property was auctioned off in 1869. The Gothic dining room was hung

[37] *Dictionary, p. 791.*
[38] *Christopher Holford,* A Chat about the Broderers' Company, *London, George Allen & Sons, 1910, pp. 185–8.*

105. Design for a president's chair, submitted by 'Cabinet-maker'. From the 'Short-Ends Corner' of *The Furniture Gazette*, 19 October 1878

DESIGN FOR A PRESIDENT'S CHAIR.   [*See p. 278.*

with paintings and engravings of past and present members (fig.102). The members sat around the table on reproductions of the Glastonbury chair (fig.32), carved with a gridiron symbol and their initials, and ate nothing but beefsteaks. They took it in turns to sit in the President's chair, which was another, larger, antiquarian confection. The Duke of Leinster is reported to have overbalanced in the President's chair and fallen into the grate on one occasion, to the accompaniment of loud laughter from the other members.[39]

The next chapter will show how the international exhibitions of the later nineteenth century stimulated the production of heavily carved

[39] *Walter Arnold*, The Life and Death of the Sublime Society of Beefsteaks, *London, Bradbury, Evans, & Co., 1871*, passim.

106. Thomas Dowsett, first Mayor of Southend-on-Sea (elected 1892), seated in the mayoral chair designed and made by Mr E. Wright of Southend for the Council Chamber in 1893. Southend Museums Service

[40] Cabinet Maker and Art Furnisher, *vol. viii, no. 87 (1 September 1887)*. Annual Report of the National Library of Wales, *1988–9*. Iorwerth C. Peate, *Guide to the collection of Welsh bygones, Cardiff, National Museum of Wales, 1929, p. 54*. On the eighteenth- and nineteenth-century revival of the Eisteddfodau cf. Prys Morgan, 'From a Death to a View: The Hunt for the Welsh Past in the Romantic Period' in Hobsbawm and Ranger.

[41] For an account of Rogers see Allwood.

ceremonial and commemorative chairs in historic styles. These chairs were also produced for local exhibitions and competitions, like the Welsh Eisteddfodau or congresses of bards. Tradition dictated that each year's victor be rewarded with a bardic chair, usually elaborately carved for the occasion by a local maker. The mishmash of historical styles and national motifs used in fig.103 is fairly representative. Collections of such chairs can be found in both the National Library of Wales and the Welsh Folk Museum.[40] Some Victorian societies also continued to commission one-off chairs, like the Tarporley Hunt Chair of 1862, a virtuoso piece of carving by the celebrated William Gibbs Rogers (1792–1875) (fig.104).[41]

There were also many more standard chairs, produced to satisfy the demands of an ever-expanding market. The most popular type was largely inspired by the Coronation Chair (fig.47), with a nod in the direction of other historic examples such as the Coventry chair (fig.71). The *Furniture Gazette* illustrated a design for a 'president's chair' of this kind in 1878 (fig.105). It suggested that it could be constructed 'at a tolerably low figure', which would be reduced still further by leaving the mouldings uncarved. The popularity of this kind of design is attested by surviving

SPENCER'S No. A. DESIGN.

Covered with Leather or Velvet.

SPENCER'S No. B. DESIGN.

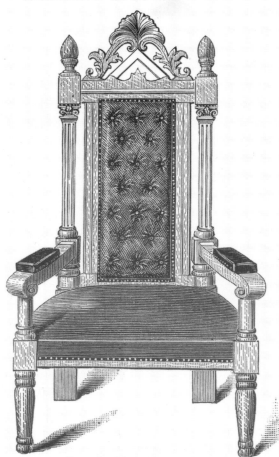

Covered with Velvet or Leather.

Chairs.

			£	s.	d.
Set of 3 for W.M., S.W., and J.W., solid Oak, upholstered in Utrecht velvet	..	..	10	10	0
,, ,, with Columns and carved capitals, Ionic, Doric and Corinthian, leather or velvet	15	15	0
,, ,, superior, B design, as above	22	10	0
,, ,, ,, A design, richly carved	27	10	0

Either of these patterns, with arms richly carved, £2 per set extra.

chairs in churches and council chambers all over the country (fig.106). Studio portraits and advertisements in the furniture trade papers indicate that they found a further use in the photographer's studio.[42] Some makers actually found it worth their while to produce readymade ceremonial chairs (fig.107): no doubt these were also supplied with engraved plaques or other personalising touches as required.

107. Masonic chairs, from a catalogue of masonic regalia produced by Spencer & Co, Great Queen Street, London, in about 1895

42 *Allwood.*

CHAPTER V

COMMEMORATIVE CHAIRS

Chairs made to commemorate a particular person, institution or event form a further category. These were usually intended for presentation and display, rarely for actual use. Thus in a sense these are the ultimate ceremonial chairs: objects which have moved beyond their apparent function to become purely symbolic. Freed from considerations of utility and comfort, their designers could concentrate on lavishing appropriate ornament and inscriptions on throne-like structures. The chosen material might also highlight their symbolism: British oak was especially popular because of its durability and patriotic associations. In some cases the availability of a particular material, like timbers from a famous ship, actually provided the occasion for the chair's manufacture.

The chair as relic

Where did the idea of the commemorative chair come from? We have already seen many thrones and other seats of authority which have been preserved through the centuries for their original purpose. Evidently the age and associations of, say, the Coronation Chair help to underline the authority of its occupant. Other chairs have also been cherished for their associations but to a rather different end: through the accidents of ownership or usage, even the humblest seat can become the secular equivalent of a holy relic. The romantic associations with King Charles the Martyr which grew up around the Juxon chair (fig.59) helped to ensure its preservation. Interestingly enough, an early reference to a 'relic-chair' comes just six years after the king's execution. The playwright Ben Jonson's chair was listed as an attraction at the Jonson's Head tavern in the Strand in 1655.[1] The idea is probably much older. The Commonwealth Inventories of the royal collections, made after Charles I's execution, list several pieces of furniture and textiles which had apparently been kept as relics, including a bed of Henry VIII's with its original hangings, and 'one little old Chaire of Crimson vellvett which was Queen Elizabeths much decayed'.[2]

The Romantic movement greatly boosted the cult of such mementoes. When the Polish Princess Isabel Czartoryska visited Shakespeare's birthplace in Stratford-upon-Avon in 1790, she was especially struck by an old oak chair associated with the playwright. She had to pay twenty guineas to add it to her collection of historic souvenirs, as the existing owner derived 'great profit' from it. 'Everybody who came to visit her house paid well for the tiniest fragments and splinters cleft from the chair, which they later set in rings and medallions.' The princess was only able to buy the back and seat, which she encased somewhat incongruously in a neo-classical chair (fig.108).[3] The legs had to be left for the owner's grand-daughter, who regarded Shakespeare as 'a sort of deity, or at least some superhuman creature' and was very upset by the sale. 'She jumped onto the chair and with great passion she tried to hold it, first with her arms and legs and finally even with her teeth. She moaned strangely and despairingly. Finally blood issued from her mouth and nose and she fell, limp and unconscious, by the chair.'

Mercifully, this was an extreme rather than a typical reponse. It was left to the Victorians to realise the pathetic possibilities of the chair to their

[1] Wit and Drollery, *1655, p. 79, quoted in Jacob Larwood and John Camden Hotten,* The History of Signboards, *London, Hotten, 1866, p. 66.*

[2] *Jervis, p. 300.*

[3] *Zygulski.*

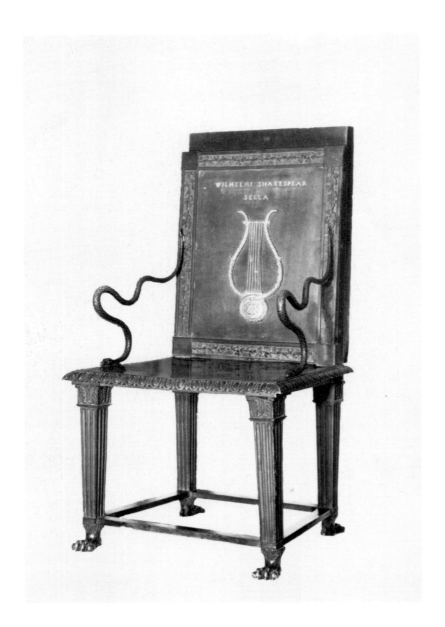

108. Shakespeare's chair. The seat and back of an oak chair purchased in 1790 from Shakespeare's heirs in Stratford-upon-Avon by Princess Isabel Czartoryska, who transformed them into a neo-classical chair. Princess Czartoryski Foundation, National Museum, Cracow

fullest extent, by using an empty seat to symbolise the aching void created by the death or absence of its regular occupant. One of the earliest and most popular examples of this phenomenon was Eliza Cook's poem to a dead mother's *Old Arm-Chair* (1836), whose opening verse runs:

> 'I love it, I love it; and who shall dare
> To chide me for loving that old arm-chair?
> I've treasured it long as a sainted prize;
> I've bedewed it with tears, and embalmed it with sighs.
> 'Tis bound by a thousand bands to my heart;
> Not a tie will break, not a link will start.
> Would ye learn the spell? – a mother sat there;
> And a sacred thing is that old arm-chair.'

Again, shortly after Charles Dickens' death in June 1870, his friend Luke Fildes made a drawing of his library at Gad's Hill entitled *The*

109. Detail of *The Empty Chair, Gad's Hill – Ninth of June 1870* by Luke Fildes. Heal archive

THE EMPTY CHAIR. GAD'S HILL—NINTH OF JUNE 1870

Empty Chair. It was published in *The Graphic* that Christmas and 'such still was the national grief at Dickens' death that thousands of the prints were put in frames and hung on the walls of the homes of Britain' (fig.109).[4]

A similar feeling for the sentimental possibilities of the inanimate object inspired George Godwin's collection of 'Suggestive Furniture'. Godwin (1815–88) was an architect and a pioneering editor of *The Builder*, especially concerned with improving working-class housing conditions (fig.110). In his house at 6 Cromwell Place, South Kensington, he assembled more than thirty chairs and other items of furniture associated with celebrities, including William Shakespeare, Sir Walter Raleigh, Charles II, Dr Watts, Napoleon, Trollope, Thackeray, Landseer, Dickens, Rossetti and Mrs Browning. He described his 'little collection' in two articles in *The Builder*, claiming that it was 'not without interest in the minds of those who admit the value of associations. This is a theme which might be the excuse for an essay, and it would not be difficult to show, if it were necessary, the importance attaching to suggestive memorials of those who have taught or delighted the world, and that amongst such materials the chair habitually used must hold a high place.' Others evidently agreed, as he referred to the 'enthusiastic citizen of the United States' who had asked him to name his own price for the Shakespeare chair,[5] and to the comment of the 'eminent author of *Palm Leaves*' that 'we have often heard of "talking

[4] *L.V. Fildes*, Luke Fildes, R.A.: A Victorian Painter, *London, Michael Joseph, 1968, p. 16. The original is in the Dickens' House Museum, while the chair itself is in the Museum of London.*

[5] *This was not the chair in Poland. Inevitably, hopeful antiquarians have imaginatively manipulated scanty evidence in attempts to link several chairs with the great playwright. Yet another is described in Fred Roe and F. Gordon Roe, 'Shakespeare's chair?',* Connoisseur, *vol. cvi, no. 7 (July 1940).*

110. Photograph of George Godwin used to illustrate his obituary in *The Builder*, 4 February 1888

tables"; these are in truth speaking chairs'.[6] Godwin tried hard to establish a proper provenance for each piece. Many modern examples were obtained through friends at the Society of Antiquaries, and its convivial offshoot the Society of Noviomagus (fig.100). The earlier chairs presented greater difficulties, and the illustrations (figs.111, 112) suggest he was sometimes over-optimistic. The chair from Hever Castle, for instance, which he bought dreaming 'without much fear of being wrong, that Anna Bullen, poor lady, often sat in it, while King Henry VIII made love to her' looks like a made-up piece, possibly incorporating a genuine panel of about 1540.[7] The collection was auctioned off after his death and most of the chairs have now disappeared. The antiquarian novelist Lord Lytton's 'Jacobean' caned chair, which is actually late seventeenth century and from the Dutch East Indies, now belongs to the National Trust and is at Wightwick Manor, Wolverhampton,[8] while the library chair associated with John Gay (1685–1732) is in the V&A. This had genuine connections with the poet's family, although the poems 'discovered' in a secret drawer in 1818 were probably a literary hoax.[9]

[6] The Builder, *vol. xxxvi, nos. 1834, p. 327 & 1870, p. 1265 (30 March and 7 December 1878). Godwin's collection is discussed at greater length in Graham 1990.*

[7] *Rogers, Chapman & Thomas, 18 April 1888.*

[8] Country Life, *vol. clxxxiv, no. 45 (Nov. 8, 1990), correspondence on p. 146.*

[9] *W.A. Thorpe, 'The Barnstaple Chair',* Devon & Cornwall Queries, *vol. xxvi, part v (Jan. 1955), p. 134.*

SUGGESTIVE FURNITURE.

111. Part of George Godwin's furniture collection. From left to right, the chairs originally belonged to Theodore Hook, Bulwer Lytton, Shakespeare and John Gay. From *The Builder*, 30 March 1878

SUGGESTIVE FURNITURE.

112. More of George Godwin's collection. From left to right, the chairs originally belonged to Anne Boleyn, Mrs Siddons, Lord Byron and Lady Morgan; the pole screen was Dr Johnson's. From *The Builder*, 7 December 1878

113. Chair made from the timbers of Sir Francis Drake's ship, the *Golden Hind*. Presented to the Bodleian Library, Oxford, in 1662. Carved oak, with engraved steel plaques

Early examples

The first purpose-made commemorative chair is apparently the example presented to the Bodleian Library in 1662, not long after the first references to 'relic-chairs' listed above (fig.113). This was made from the timbers of the *Golden Hind*, the ship on which Francis Drake sailed around the world and was knighted by Elizabeth I at Deptford on 4 April 1581. The ship herself also received a hero's welcome: one contemporary jested that she should be hoisted bodily onto the stump of the steeple of old St Paul's Cathedral, in place of the missing spire. Instead, and traditionally at the insistence of the Queen, she was laid up in dock at Deptford. Fitted out as a supper and drinking room, the *Golden Hind* attracted large numbers of visitors, but by the mid-seventeenth century she was literally worn out and had to be broken up. The Bodleian chair was presented by the storekeeper at Deptford dockyard, John Davies of Camberwell. The design is striking, and suggests a Flemish source: it may be compared to a chair in Trinity Hall, Aberdeen dated 1661 (fig.74). The original turned acorn or bobbin-shaped feet have been sawn off but can be seen in an early illustration:[10]

[10] *Rowley Lascelles*, The University and City of Oxford, *London, Sherwood Neely & Jones, 1821, p. 135.*

114. Tea caddy made from the wood of the Shakespeare mulberry. Dated 1758 and signed by the maker, George Cooper of Stratford-upon-Avon. W.16–1981

11 For the Bodleian chair cf. Bodleian Quarterly Record, vol. iv (1923–5), p. 45. BQR, vol. ii (1920–2), p. 127–8, p. 151, mentions two of the other chairs. There are photographs of these in the library's records. The others were lot 431, Christies' South Kensington, Carpets, Decorative Objects and Furniture, 2 May 1990.
12 Michael Hunter, 'The cabinet institutionalised: the Royal Society's Repository and its Background', The Origins of Museums: the cabinet of curiosities in sixteenth and seventeenth century Europe, ed. Oliver Impey and Arthur Macgregor, Oxford, Clarendon Press, 1985, pp. 147–58.

there is evidence of clumsy repairs but not of any substantial alterations. Bobbins evidently also originally hung from the centre of each arch, and three surmounted the back (two have been replaced). Four other very similar chairs have been recorded. These are larger and not so well carved, and some features of the design have been rationalised in a way which suggests that they are copies made for the nineteenth-century antiquarian market, like fig.34.[11] The Bodleian may now seem a strange home for such an object, but many early libraries housed cabinets of curiosities, intended to promote science and encourage visitors. The chair joined existing collections of coins and ethnographic material and other more miscellaneous attractions such as Guy Fawkes' lantern.[12] Finally, it is worth noting that although the chair is larger than average and obviously not intended for ordinary use, its identity is not immediately clear. There is none of the elaborately symbolic decoration found on later commemorative chairs, although a steel plaque on the back is engraved with Latin and English verses by Abraham Cowley recording the gift.

Given the right associations, raw wood could be as emotive as ships' timbers. Stratford-upon-Avon became a Shakespeare shrine well before Princess Isabel Czartoryska's visit in 1790, and one place of pilgrimage was a mulberry tree in the garden at New Place, reputedly planted by the playwright. In 1756 the owner of the house, the Reverend Francis Gastrell, became so infuriated by the constant stream of visitors that he had the tree cut down. Local entrepreneurs swiftly established a profitable trade in small mulberrywood souvenirs, which one suspects continued long after the original source dried up (fig.114). These were popular with tourists, and for presentation by the local corporation. As organiser of the 1769

115. The President's Chair of the
Shakespeare Club. Mahogany with
composition medallion and leather seat.
From the Shakespeare Temple in the grounds
of David Garrick's villa at Hampton,
Middlesex. Thought to have been designed
by William Hogarth in about 1756. Folger
Shakespeare Library, Washington DC

Shakespeare Jubilee in Stratford, the actor David Garrick was presented
with a casket containing the freedom of the borough, which is now in the
British Museum. His medallion and wand of office were also made from
Shakespeare's mulberry. Throughout his life he was evidently deluged with
mulberrywood souvenirs: some were handed on to fellow-actors and
friends, but even so the sale after his widow's death in 1823 included no
fewer than five uncarved and 'Well-Authenticated Blocks from the
Celebrated Mulberry Tree of Shakespeare'.[13] He also had a large
commemorative chair in the Shakespeare Temple of his riverside villa at
Hampton (fig.115). According to Horace Walpole, this was designed for
Garrick as president of the Shakespeare Club by William Hogarth. It is
certainly much more sophisticated than most of the chairs in this chapter:
some elements of the ornament are close to the designs of Gravelot, and
suggest Hogarth's own early career in silver engraving. The design is
elaborately symbolic. Twining serpents, symbolising Wisdom, gaze
admiringly at a portrait medallion of Shakespeare, and there are also
references both to his Tragedies (the dagger, sword, and the mask which

13 *Christian Deelman*, The Great
Shakespeare Jubilee, *London, Michael Joseph,
1964, ch. 2.*

116. Chair made from the timbers of the Dutch fleet, captured at the Battle of Camperdown in 1797. Oak, with an engraved silver plaque. National Maritime Museum, Greenwich

seems to be a portrait of Garrick himself in the trophy surmounting the back) and his Comedies (there are satyr masks, buskins and cloven feet on the legs, a position which reflects their less dignified place in the artistic hierarchy).[14] Walpole claimed the portrait medallion was carved in Shakespeare mulberrywood: the present example is made from composition, but may be a replacement.

Hearts of oak

From about 1800, commemorative chairs began to be produced in much larger quantities, often as a patriotic response to international events. Three in the National Maritime Museum seem at first to be handsome but conventional library chairs. Closer inspection reveals that the arms are miniature cannon barrels, and there are anchor and crown motifs on the back. The top and bottom back rails are carved with the inscription 'This wood was part of Adml. De Winter's fleet captur'd by Adml. Duncan Octr. 11 1797'. A silver plaque fixed to the seat of one chair (fig.116) is inscribed 'This chair was made for Admiral Edward O'Bryen, who

14 Rococo, pp. 67–8.

117. Chair made from the wood of the Waterloo Elm, presented to George IV by John George Children in 1821. Made by Thomas Chippendale the Younger. Royal Collection

commanded His Majesty's ship *Monarch* in the battle of Camperdown; at his death it came into the possession of Admiral the Marquis of Thomond by whom it was presented to Robert Earl of Camperdown AD 1847'. Both Rear-Admiral Edward O'Bryen (1754?–1808) and Admiral Adam Duncan, later Viscount Duncan of Camperdown (1731–1804) played a distinguished part in the defeat of the Dutch fleet at the battle of Camperdown. Presumably the chairs were made shortly afterwards for officers who had taken part in the action; other examples are recorded. The chair shown in fig.117 is more fully documented, being one of three made from the elm tree which marked Wellington's command post at Waterloo. This was felled in 1818 for much the same reasons as Shakespeare's mulberry: the farmer on whose land it stood was tired of the damage done to his corn by tourists. John George Children, Fellow of the Royal Society and the Society of Antiquaries and Librarian of the Department of Antiquities in the British Museum, happened to be making a tour of the battlefield and immediately purchased the timber. In 1821 he presented a Waterloo Elm armchair, made by Thomas Chippendale the Younger, to George IV. Again, the form is conventional but the decoration

118. A bishop's chair made from the timbers of HMS *Téméraire*. Oak, about 1850, designed by Beatson for St Paul's, Rotherhithe. Now in the parish church of St Mary's, Rotherhithe

is elaborately symbolic. It includes military trophies, a scene showing the British lion bestriding a fallen enemy colour before the village of Waterloo, and a grandiloquent Latin inscription honouring the king. There are two more Waterloo Elm chairs by unidentified makers at Apsley House and Belvoir Castle, and various other items have been recorded.[15]

Some of Nelson's warships remained in service long after the Napoleonic era. Even in their decay they retained a certain glamour in the popular imagination. J.M.W. Turner sketched the *Téméraire*, veteran of Trafalgar, on her way to the shipbreaker's yard on an autumn evening in 1838: his great painting of *The Fighting Téméraire tugged to her last berth* would be hailed by Ruskin as 'the most pathetic of subjects not involving human pain that ever was painted'. The shipbreaker, John Beatson of Rotherhithe, was a local churchwarden. When a chapel of ease was built near his yard in 1850, he presented some *Téméraire* timber to the architect, a rather obscure relative of his also called Beatson. It was used to make two

119. A view of the staircase in the study at Abbotsford, by William Gibb, showing the Robroyston chair. From Mary Monica Maxwell-Scott, *Abbotsford: the personal relics and antiquarian treasures of Sir Walter Scott*, London, 1893

solid but rather clumsy Gothic bishop's chairs (fig.118), a communion table decorated with a rope moulding and some altar rails. After the chapel of St Paul's fell into disuse in the late 1950s the table and chairs were moved to the mother church of St Mary's, Rotherhithe.[16]

Enough chairs, boxes, and other commemorative items survive to suggest that there was a large market for memorabilia of this kind, and that supplies were still available even in the early twentieth century.[17] The Manchester firm of Goodall, Lamb and Heighway, for instance, produced a very ambitious catalogue in 1904 which offered anything from a fully fitted ship's cabin to a smoker's companion in oak and copper from HMS *Foudroyant*. It also provided a detailed history of this ship, whose chief claim to fame was a brief period as Nelson's flagship in 1799–1800. After a long career as a guardship at Devonport, she had been wrecked off Blackpool in 1897. It is not clear how many of these designs were ever actually made up. Many were copies of older pieces, some with naval associations like the Camperdown chairs (fig.116): the Regency style was after all fashionable as well as appropriate to the material.[18]

[16] *Revd Edward Josselyn Beck,* Memorials to serve for a history of the Parish of St Mary Rotherhithe*, Cambridge, University Press, 1907, p. 74–5, and information supplied by the Rector of St Mary's.*

[17] *For instance, apart from the chairs discussed here the National Maritime Museum have a Bellerephon chair made c. 1836, a Victory chair made c. 1922, and some Téméraire items.*

[18] Foudroyant.

120. The Battle Abbey Throne. Oak, about 1817. Made for the Great Hall at Battle Abbey, probably in the workshops of George Bullock and to the design of Richard Bridgens. W.56–1980

The antiquarian urge

Commemorative chairs have an obvious appeal for the historically minded, and the growing fashion for antiquarian interiors in the early nineteenth century undoubtedly assisted their popularity. Hitherto these chairs had been made in styles which reflected contemporary furniture fashion, albeit with varying degrees of sophistication. At this date, and in line with the developments described in earlier chapters, their designers began to feel historic styles were more suitable. It seems especially appropriate that an early example of such a chair was made for Sir Walter Scott, the individual who did most to create the fashion for the antiquarian interior, and that it is still at Abbotsford (fig.119). The Robroyston chair was made by John Stirling of Kirkcudbrightshire on the orders of Joseph Train, an exciseman and poet who often supplied Scott with legends and antiquities. The wood used came from the ends of rafters found in the ruins of the house of Robroyston, where Sir William Wallace was executed by the English in 1305. Train recorded how 'the symbolic chair' was shipped off to Scott 'in the midst the town-band playing "Scots wha hae wi' Wallace bled" and

121. The *Champion Chair* by Edmund Hutchinson of High Wycombe, shown at the Great Exhibition of 1851. The carving was the work of his son, Edmund Junior. Wycombe Local History and Chair Museum

surrounded by thousands'. Scott was enchanted by his gift, writing to Train in May 1822 'I found the curious chair which your kindness destined for me safe here on my return from Abbotsford. It is *quite* invaluable to me who am filling up an addition to my house in the country with things of that antique nature'.[19] The form was taken from a late seventeenth-century chair in the Palace of Hamilton, but the decoration was a riot of Scottish symbolism, including rocks, heather, thistles, warhorns, claymores, and 'The Harp of the North'. Another early example of the new mood is equally, if not so overtly, patriotic. The Battle Abbey Throne (fig.120) was designed as part of an extensive medievalising building programme at Battle Abbey, the monastery built on the site of the Battle of Hastings by William the Conqueror. The owner, Sir Godfrey Vassal Webster, carried out the work between about 1810 and 1822, apparently prompted by the desire to restore a national shrine at a time of international crisis. The massive oak throne in the Gothic style stood on a dais below a canopy at the west end of the fifteenth-century Great Hall, beneath a huge painting of the Battle of Hastings by F.W. Wilkin, a pupil of Benjamin West. It is thought to have been made in the workshops of the cabinet-maker George Bullock along with other furniture for the

[19] *Wainwright, p. 198.*

122. Two commemorative chairs shown at the Great Exhibition of 1851. To the left, Shacklock's *Heraldic Chair*. To the right, a chair made by Collinson of Doncaster from two-thousand-year-old oak. From G.W. Yapp, *Furniture Upholstery and House Decoration*, London, about 1876

abbey, probably to a design by Richard Bridgens. It is not a straight copy of an old chair, but an early nineteenth-century essay in the use of Gothic forms and motifs.

The age of exhibitions

The great international exhibitions of art and industry certainly stimulated the production of commemorative chairs during the second half of the nineteenth century. Show-piece chairs were specially made for these events in order to advertise their makers' technical virtuosity. Like the massive sideboards which were also popular for this purpose, they lent themselves to the kind of elaborate carving on a historic or symbolic theme which was greatly prized at this time. Perhaps the best-known carver working in this vein was William Gibbs Rogers, an example of whose work has already been illustrated (fig.104). There were many others, notably at Warwick (William Cookes, James Willcox and Thomas Kendall) and at Newcastle-upon-Tyne (William Stamp, Thomas Tweedy and Gerrard Robinson).[20] Such a chair was by its nature not suited to the average customer's needs, but with skilful promotion it was far from being a white

[20] *Allwood.*

ARM CHAIR.

123. Armchair from a suite of Irish historic furniture, shown at the Great Exhibition of 1851. Made by Arthur J. Jones, Son & Co. of Dublin from Irish bog yew. From the maker's *Description of a suite of sculptured decorative furniture*, Dublin, 1853

elephant. If no wealthy patron proved interested in buying it, the maker could generate further publicity once the exhibition was over by presenting it to some notable person or institution, or displaying it in his showrooms, or even raffling it if all else failed.

The Great Exhibition held in London in 1851, for instance, included at least nine 'show-piece' chairs. None of them were the work of the top-flight carvers mentioned above, but rather of obscure provincial makers evidently hoping to compete in the same field. Carving after all required time and skill rather than a large or elaborately equipped workshop. The women who produced the chair in fig.43 were evidently not working on a large commercial scale. Probably the best known of the makers showing commemorative chairs in 1851 was Edmund Hutchinson from High Wycombe, the centre of the British chair-making industry. His oak *Champion Chair* (fig.121) was upholstered in silk velvet and the elaborate carved decoration by his son Edmund Junior included shells, rococo scrolls and national emblems.[21] The celebrated Glastonbury 'Abbot's Chair', and its numerous nineteenth-century copies (fig.34), were discussed in chapter II. John Budge of Wells showed both a full-sized oak copy and a miniature ivory model.[22] John Carmichael of Workington showed an oak armchair 'of novel design' which was carved with birds and foliage and had two rampant lions for arms, cut from the root of oak. The crimson velvet upholstery was embroidered by George Haines of Chelsea.[23] G. Shacklock of Bolsover, Derbyshire, showed a highly patriotic *Heraldic Chair* (fig.122), which was carved from native oak with the heraldic devices of Queen Victoria's ancestors, from Edward the Confessor downwards. It failed to catch the Queen's eye as Shacklock had hoped, so he raffled it. The Revd John Hamilton Gray, rural dean of Bolsover, and his daughter Maria, wife of John Anstruther Thomson of Charleton in Fife, held the winning ticket, and the chair is still at Charleton.[24] Also visible in fig.122 is a chair in fossil oak by George Croyser Collinson of Doncaster. The wood had been found in the river Don at Arksey, near Doncaster, in about 1848 and was supposed to be 2000 years old. The decoration included oak branches, leaves, acorns and the crest of the owner, Mr Chadwick of Arksey.[25] W. Jancowski of York also hoped that his state chair, which was upholstered in crimson velvet and embroidered with various Royal and national emblems, would be purchased for the Royal Collection, but its later history is not known.[26] There were three Irish chairs carved from bog-wood, examples of a national specialism developed to appeal to both the tourist trade and to patriotic local patrons.[27] J. Curran & Sons of Lisburn showed a

[21] Section III, class 26, no. 22. See also Allwood.

[22] Catalogue, *Section III, class 26, no. 219.*

[23] Catalogue, *Section III, class 26, no. 114.*

[24] Catalogue, *Section III, class 26, no. 78.* See William Kay, 'Charleton, Fife. The home of Baron and Baroness St Clair Bonde', Country Life, vol. clxxxiv, no. 8 (Feb. 22, 1990), p. 98.

[25] Catalogue, *Section III, class 26, no. 90.*

[26] Catalogue, *Section III, class 19, no. 48.* Illustrated Exhibitor, 1851, p. 238.

[27] Details of this and the related arbutus marquetry pieces from Killarney are given in Brian Austen, Tunbridge Ware and related European Decorative Woodwares, London, W. Foulsham & Co. Ltd., 1989, chapter 13.

124. The *Adderley Chair*, shown at the Great Exhibition of 1851. South African stink-wood: designed by Thomas Baines and carved by Joseph Hart. Presented to Charles Bowyer Adderley MP in 1849 by the inhabitants of Grahamstown, South Africa. Private collection

sculptured and perforated armchair from the antique, made of black Irish bog-oak from Montagh's Moss, with crimson silk velvet upholstery. 'Three poor working men' made it specifically for the exhibition, over eight months of 'unlimited hours'. A block of the seasoned wood and pencil designs by the self-taught makers were also shown.[28] The two other Irish entries were rich in symbolic decoration. Dawson Bell of Belfast showed a devotional chair in bog oak, upholstered in needlework and carved with shamrocks, wolf-hounds, figures of Hope and Plenty, and the harp of Brian Boroihme, complete with silver strings.[29] The most elaborate variation on this theme was the suite of bog yew furniture 'illustrative of Irish history and antiquities' made by Arthur J. Jones of Dublin. The lavish catalogue claimed 'the main characteristic of the whole is its wonderful PICTURESQUENESS . . . the spirit of the whole is as intensely national, as the method of display is original and ingenious'. The chair illustrated (fig.123) is plain compared to some of the other pieces, although it is surmounted by the ancient shield of Ireland and busts of ancient Irish

[28] Catalogue, *Section III, class 26, no. 215. The chair is illustrated in* The Illustrated Exhibitor, *1851, p. 143.*

[29] Catalogue, *Section III, class 26, no. 212.*

125. One of a set of four armchairs shown at the Great Exhibition of 1851 and presented to Queen Victoria. Designed by Ferdinand Rothbart and made by Thomas Hoffmeister and Thomas Behrens of Coburg. W.10–1967

warriors and has 'elbow-rests . . . formed by chimeras, supported on the legs and paws of Irish wolf-dogs'.[30]

This is not an exhaustive list. Other British chairs could be described as semi-commemorative, such as the two walnut chairs inset with porcelain plaques of Victoria and Albert shown by Henry Eyles of Bath.[31] There were also commemorative chairs from British dependencies: both Read and Meakins and J.& W. Hilton of Montreal showed chairs with upholstery embroidered by the ladies of Montreal, intended for presentation to the Queen.[32] A still more elaborate presentation piece was the stinkwood armchair given by the inhabitants of Grahamstown in South Africa to Charles Bowyer Adderley MP, later Lord Norton. The inscription on the South African gold plaque recorded that this was 'in gratitude for his efforts in opposing the Material Scheme for making the Colony a Penal Settlement and for his generous defence of their just Rights and Privileges as British subjects in the House of Commons'. The carvings of characteristic South African scenes were designed by Thomas Baines and carved by Joseph Hart (fig.124). The chair is still in the family's possession at Fillongley Hall, near Coventry.[33] Some foreign manufacturers showed chairs which, if not commemorative, were certainly on a

[30] Catalogue, *Section III, class 26, no. 78* and Arthur J. Jones, Son, & Co., Description of a suite of sculptured decorative furniture, *Dublin, Hodges & Smith, 1853.*

[31] Catalogue, *Section III, class 26, no. 50. The two chairs were acquired by the V&A in the 1950s, with an accompanying table (W. 31–1953, Circ. 35–1958, W. 40–1952).*

[32] Catalogue, *Canada, nos. 115A and 123. The Hilton chair is illustrated in Yapp, pl. xxiv.*

[33] Catalogue, *South Africa, no. 57. See also Thorpe, and Gervase Jackson-Stops, 'Fillongley Hall, Coventry, Warwickshire. The seat of Lord and Lady Norton', Country Life, vol. clxxxiii, no. 29 (July 20, 1989), p. 67.*

126. The London Bridge Chair. Oak, with a stone seat. Made by John Ovenston to the design of John Rennie and presented to the Worshipful Company of Fishmongers in 1848 to commemorate the return of their freeman, Baron Rothschild, as the first Jewish MP. From J. Wrench Towse, *The Worshipful Company of Fishmongers of London*, London, 1907

ceremonial scale. The four massively architectural oak thrones designed by Ferdinand Rothbart (1823–99) and made by Thomas Hoffmeister and Thomas Behrens of Coburg were presented to Queen Victoria and reached the V&A in the 1960s (fig.125).[34] The overwhelming impression remains distinctly ponderous: despite the high standard of workmanship and the manifest patriotism of the makers, these were poorly designed objects, heavily burdened with over-naturalistic and inappropriate decoration. It is only fair to point out that this was also the verdict of many contemporary viewers, including the judges: none of these chairs were included amongst the objects acquired from the exhibition for the nascent V&A with the aim of encouraging good modern design.

Celebrations and disasters

The presentation of a commemorative chair might mark almost any kind of occasion in the nineteenth century. An example at Fishmongers' Hall, for instance, was given to the Company in 1848 by their tenant, John Hall, to commemorate the return of Baron Rothschild (himself a Fishmonger) as the first Jewish MP (fig.126). It had been made of timber and stone from the foundations of old London Bridge, apparently some years earlier: an inscription indicates that the Revd Wm John Jolliffe, Curate of Colmar in Hampshire, rescued the materials in July 1832 when a new bridge was being built to the designs of John Rennie (1761–1821). The chair was

[34] Catalogue, *Zollverein, no. 773.*

127. The Scoresby chair. Oak with a brass plaque. Made by W. Bayes and Son of Liverpool from the timbers of the *Royal Charter* and presented to the widow of the Revd William Scoresby in 1861. Presented to the parish church of St Mary, Whitby by Dr Scoresby-Jackson in 1922. From a newspaper cutting in the Heal Archive dated 17 January 1863

made by John Ovenston, a cabinet-maker and upholsterer at 72 Great Titchfield Street off Oxford Street, supposedly to Rennie's design. The seat is highly polished stone, carved with another inscription; the square bases of the legs represent the foundation stone of the old bridge; the supports of the seat and arms are 'fac-similes of the several bridges built by Messrs Jolliffe and Banks over the Thames'; the cross bars on the back represent Waterloo, Southwark, Old and New London Bridges, and the arms of the City of London appear on the cresting. The Fishmongers also have a snuff-box made as part of the same commission.[35]

Another chair (fig.127) was presented in 1861 to the widow of the Revd William Scoresby DD, FRS (1789–1857), a Whitby man who was a distinguished seaman and scientist as well as a clergyman. The chair was made from the timbers of the *Royal Charter*, the iron-screw steamer on which Scoresby sailed to Australia in 1856 at the invitation of the Liverpool Shipowners' Association, to establish the effect of the new iron ships on their compasses and to calculate the necessary adjustments.[36] The ship was wrecked off Anglesey on a later voyage in 1859. In an appalling accident which attracted much press attention, 386 of the 405 passengers and crew were drowned. The 'owners of the vessel and other friends connected with the ship-owning and underwriting interests of the Port of

[35] *J. Wrench Towse*, Worshipful Company of Fishmongers of London: a short account of portraits, pictures, plate, etc., etc., in the possession of the company, *London, William Clowes and Sons, 1907, pp. 45–6 and* Court Minute Book *of the Fishmongers' Company in Guildhall Library, 9 March 1848.*

[36] *Robert Edmund Scoresby-Jackson,* The life of William Scoresby, *London, 1861, pp. 364–85.*

128. Two chairs made from the timbers of HMS *Royal George* and upholstered in red leather. Designed by Henry Whitaker of Greenholme, Burley, near Otley and made by Thomas Wood Jr., 1839–41. Presented by the daughters of the designer to the National Maritime Museum

[37] *Heal, unidentified newspaper report, 17 January 1863.*

[38] *See Brigadier R.F. Johnson,* The Royal George, *London, Charles Knight & Co., 1971, p. 158 et passim.*

Liverpool' got W. Bayes & Son of Liverpool to make some of the salvage into a presentation chair.[37] It is an imposing but not especially inspired design in typical mid-Victorian taste, carved with naval motifs and a view of the wreck of the *Royal Charter* entitled 'Thou rulest the raging of the sea'. A compass and engraved brass plaque are set into the back. Both its appearance and its associations must have been rather overwhelming in a domestic setting, and in 1922 Dr Thomas Scoresby-Jackson found it a more appropriate home in the parish church.

The National Maritime Museum owns two more chairs made from the timbers of a ship: the *Royal George* (fig.128). These were completed in 1842 to a design by Henry Whitaker of Greenholme, Burley, near Otley, Yorks, and made by Thomas Wood Junior. The *Royal George* was a first rate ship of the line which had sunk in 1782 with the loss of some 900 lives while heeled over for repairs at Spithead. Several loads of timber were brought up and auctioned off in 1839–41, when the wreck was blown up as a hazard to shipping. Again, souvenirs were produced on a commercial scale, especially boxes and book-covers for sensationalist accounts of the catastrophe. The capital of Nelson's Column was cast from some of the salvaged guns.[38] The two chairs were presented to the museum by Whitaker's daughters. Unfortunately it is not clear who he was or why he felt drawn to make them. There was a professional furniture designer of the same name working around this date, whose published designs are competent, rather dull interpretations of currently fashionable styles. They include a commemorative chair, presented to the Revd Andrew of St James's, Westminster by his parishioners in 1847 (fig.129). This looks relatively comfortable compared to most of the examples in this chapter: it was made

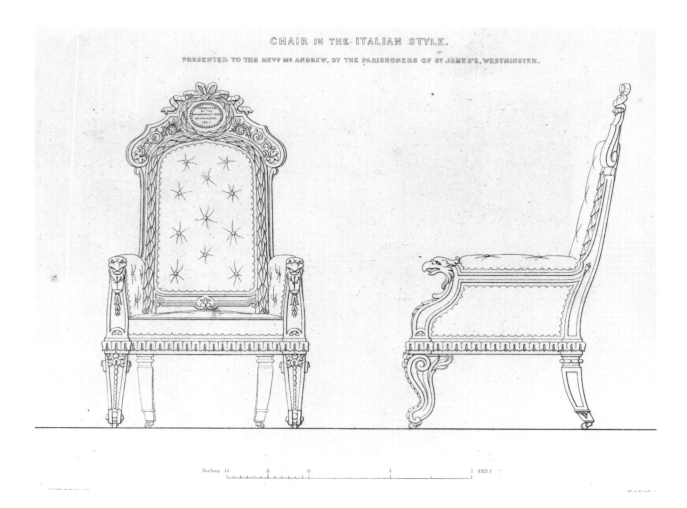

CHAIR IN THE ITALIAN STYLE.

PRESENTED TO THE REV^D MR ANDREW, BY THE PARISHIONERS OF ST JAMES'S, WESTMINSTER.

in oak by the London firm of Bantings. Whitaker also worked with Hollands.[39] The Greenwich chairs, however, suggest the obsessive fantasy of an eccentric amateur. They are of oak, inlaid with other woods, and upholstered in red leather. The construction is solid but clumsy: each separate section of the apron is fixed into the seat rail with huge screws, for instance. One has zig-zag front legs which create a curious kinetic effect from some angles but appear perfectly straight from others, cabriole back legs in the form of dolphins, and a great deal of geometric ornament. The other is even stranger. An apron of shells and leaves hangs from the seat rail, the front feet are fearsomely webbed, and each back leg is a hybrid monster, somewhere between a caterpillar and a dolphin. The badge inlaid in the back is, rather puzzlingly, that of the Guelphic Order of Hanover which was founded by the Prince Regent in 1815, long after the *Royal George* sank.

By trawling through nineteenth-century newspapers and exhibition catalogues, it would be possible to produce an enormous list of commemorative chairs. Such a task is beyond the scope of this book, but no doubt many unrecorded furniture makers would emerge, along with a great many firmly dated and documented pieces of furniture. Even this short survey has made it apparent that many of these elaborately symbolic objects had a practical underlying purpose beyond commemoration: generating publicity, either for the maker or someone else associated with their presentation. The manufacturers of High Wycombe, the centre of the British chair-making industry, were especially aware of the possibilities

129. Design for a chair in the Italian style, presented to the Revd Mr Andrew by the parishioners of St James's, Westminster in 1847. From Henry Whitaker, *Practical Cabinet-Maker and Upholsterer's Treasury of Designs*, London, 1847

[39] *Henry Whitaker, Practical cabinet maker and upholsterer's treasury of designs, house-furnishing and decorating assistant in the Grecian, Italian, Renaissance, Louis-Quatorze, Gothic, Tudor and Elizabethan Styles, London, Fisher, Son & Co., 1847, and various other publications. See also Edward Joy, 'Holland and Sons and the Furniture of Osborne House', Antiques, April 1971, pp. 580–5.*

130. Gilt armchair with tapestry upholstery made by the Royal Windsor Tapestry Manufactory and presented by them to the Duke of Albany on the occasion of his marriage in 1882. Heal Archive

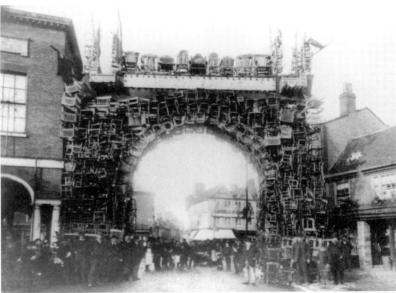

131. A triumphal arch of chairs erected at the Guild Hall, High Wycombe, on the occasion of Prince Edward's visit to Lord Beaconsfield at Hughenden in 1880. High Wycombe Central Library

offered by the commemorative chair. Ivan Sparkes has shown how manufacturers presented examples of their products to the local corporation, and to members of the Royal Family, especially on occasions such as weddings and jubilees or local visits (figs.9,121,130). They even developed a new type of street decoration to greet royal visitors: triumphal arches constructed from chairs (fig.131).[40]

CHAPTER VI

THE CEREMONIAL CHAIR IN THE TWENTIETH CENTURY

Throughout the twentieth century, ceremonial chairs have continued to be produced in quantity. Thrones and chairs of state are obviously still needed for great ceremonies such as a coronation or state opening of parliament, but the majority are to be found in courts of justice, civic chambers and other more mundane settings. Some are simply enlarged, high-backed versions of the mass-produced seats used to furnish the rest of the room (fig.132). Others have been specially commissioned for their setting (fig.133).[1] Often the details of their design and manufacture will be more readily accessible than is the case with earlier examples. The story behind one particular throne forms the basis of the next section. The exceptionally full surviving account of this commission makes it possible to re-examine some of the issues raised in earlier chapters in greater detail. It will become clear that the same traditions and expedients have continued to characterise the design and manufacture of the ceremonial chair in the twentieth century, but it will also become clear that new problems have emerged as well. The nature of these will be discussed in the final section.

The Abyssinian throne

Thrones and chairs of state make suitable items for ritual presentations between governments. Even in imperial Rome an ivory *sella curulis* was a customary gift of honour to foreign rulers.[2] In Great Britain in the twentieth century, a Speaker's Chair could be seen as an equally appropriate gift from the mother of parliamentary democracies. For instance, the British Government made and presented a series of Speakers' Chairs to its former colonies when they achieved independence. One is shown in fig.134. Earlier, in 1921, the United Kingdom branch of the Empire Parliamentary Association presented the rebuilt Canadian Parliament with a replica of Pugin's Speaker's Chair, made from old wood taken from the roof of Westminster Hall.[3] The compliment was returned when the British House of Commons was rebuilt after the Second World War. The furnishings were donated by Commonwealth countries, and included a black bean wood Speaker's Chair from Australia.[4]

In different circumstances, another type of throne might be more appropriate. In 1924, Prince Ras Tafari of Abyssinia (later Emperor Haile Selassie) visited England. The Foreign Office wanted to make some kind of presentation to commemorate the visit, and decided that 'no individual presents should be given to the Ras and to members of his suite but that His Majesty's Government should present a throne to the Abyssinian Government'. The reasons for this decision are not stated, but in the light of later developments it seems likely that it was thought that this would be cheaper and better for publicity. However, the Foreign Office had little experience of this kind of commission and soon found itself in difficulties. In July it called on the Victoria and Albert Museum for help. The museum's Director, Cecil Harcourt Smith, was at first rather cautious, not to say guarded, in his response: 'I must confess I have some misgivings about the possibility of arriving at anything in the nature of a throne which will be at once pleasing to the Abyssinians and not an outrage upon

[1] Edward H. Pinto, The Origins and History of the Worshipful Company of Furniture-Makers, London, Company, 1974 (2nd ed.).

[2] Wanscher, ch. vii.

[3] Illustrated London News April 9, 1921, pp. 482–3. (see fig 4)

[4] Sir Bryan H. Fell and K.R. Mackenzie, The Houses of Parliament, London, HMSO, 1988, pp. 45–6.

132. Detail of a design for a judge's chair produced by the Property Services Agency. Signed N.G.C. and dated 15.2.73. Archive of Art and Design

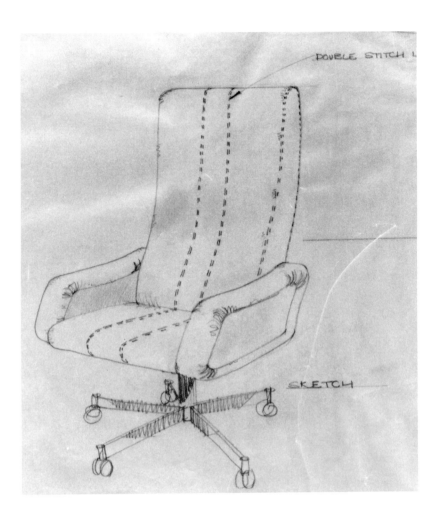

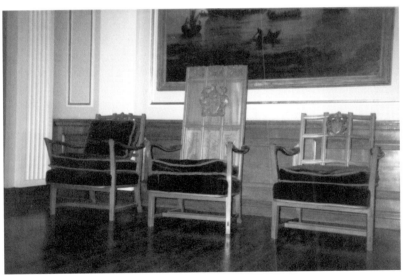

133. Master's and Wardens' Chairs of the Company of Furniture Makers. Elm, carved with the arms of the company and the furniture maker's tools. Designed and presented by Lucian Ercolani, chairman of Ercol Furniture, in 1972

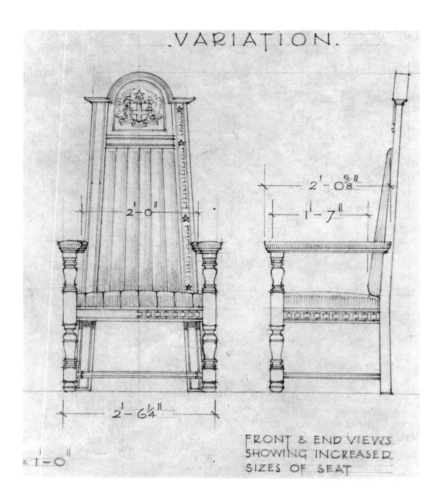

134. Design for a Speaker's Chair for the National Assembly of Ghana, produced by the Property Services Agency. Signed F.McC. and dated 16.12.57. Archive of Art and Design

135. Set of masonic armchairs, formerly in the possession of the South Middlesex Lodge. Mahogany, inlaid with lighter wood; about 1730. W.218–20–1923

136. President's Chair. Mahogany with a gilt brass finial, about 1765. From Lyon's Inn, London, a former Inn of Chancery. W.63–1911

⁵ *Nominal files in the V&A's Registry for the Emperor of Abyssinia and Sir Cecil Harcourt Smith. I am grateful to Michael Snodin for drawing these to my attention. Further references are taken from the Foreign Office files in the Public Record Office, reference FO371/10872.*

educated British taste. If, however, the matter is already decided and as this Museum is the official centre of design in industrial crafts, I suppose it should properly fall to us to undertake it.' The project was to prove a complicated one. Its progress is recorded in the extensive file in the Museum's records which forms the basis of this account.⁵

Smith sorted out some practical points at a meeting with Victor Mallet of the Foreign Office and Mr Zaphiro, Oriental Secretary at Addis Ababa. The throne was actually intended for presentation to Ras Tafari's mother Zauditu, the Empress Regent of Abyssinia. Its cost was not to exceed £350 (with another £100 allowed for packing and transport). It needed to be made of a hard wood such as teak, because of the prevalence of white ant at Addis Ababa. The upholstery would have to be in the form of a separate cushion as 'the Abyssinians suffer a good deal from the particular kind of insect that lives in wool and feeds on humans, and any sort of fixed upholstery is an invitation to them to take up their abode there'. The Foreign Office undertook to provide details of the Abyssinian royal emblems for the decoration, and later supplied a suitable Amharic inscription. They inspected some 'specimens of Official Chairs in the Museum Collections' (figs.135,136) and some 'extremely elaborate gilt

Venetian furniture which we have in store' (fig.137), and decided that the design should be 'based upon our Chippendale Masters' Chairs, so long as a sufficient amount of gilt and as much elaborate carving as would not make the design intolerable were used'. The Foreign Office asked that designs be drawn up for their approval, suggesting that 'if the throne will not be sufficiently low-seated for a short-legged oriental monarch, designs may also be prepared at the same time for a footstool to provide a means of access to the throne'.

Smith called in Laurence Turner, a London-based craftsman who worked in plaster and stone as well as wood: he was Master of the Art Workers' Guild in 1922 and published a book on *Decorative Plasterwork in Britain* in 1927.[6] Turner's first design was based on an eighteenth-century throne from a church in Cyprus, at that time in the V&A's collections (fig.138). He felt 'a combination of Oriental and Western styles' was likelier to appeal to the Abyssinians than a more purist approach. However, on 19 September 1924 the Foreign Office wrote back to Eric Maclagan (who had taken over as the V&A's Director) stating that this design was unacceptable. They felt the canopy over the throne was inappropriate 'for Abyssinia, where such things are not known and where a prejudice might exist against such an innovation. It might also be considered too

137. Two armchairs from a set of six. Venetian, third quarter of the eighteenth century. Carved and gilded wood. 537–42–1874 (now destroyed)

[6] *See Turner's obituary in the Journal of the Royal Institute of British Architects, vol. 65, no. 6 (April 1958), p. 212. There is a tea caddy made by Turner in the V&A's collections, dated 1899 (Circ. 756-b-1966).*

138. Throne (iconostasis) dated 1779, from a church in Cyprus. Vinewood and walnut, carved, painted and gilt. Formerly in the V&A's collections, and used as a model for the first design for the Abyssinian throne. 43–1905

ecclesiastical.' They pointed out that the seat needed to be roomier so the Empress could sit cross-legged and feared that 'the barbaric taste of the Abyssinians will make it advisable to gild most, if not all of the woodwork'. They also stated that as the throne would be placed in the centre of a room the workmanship on its back needed to be good as well. Turner accordingly prepared a new design, which was approved by the Foreign Office on 20 October. He worked slowly, but the finished object was eventually dispatched in August 1925 aboard HMS *Weymouth*. When it arrived the British Minister in Addis Ababa, Charles Bentinck, wrote to his superiors that he was 'a little disappointed in the Throne . . . the velvet cushion . . . has been rather crushed, and the whole gives the idea of having been done on the cheap. Considering it took over a year to make, I confess I had expected something finer. Zaphiro is also rather disappointed. Apparently they have made a mistake in the Amharic lettering.' Nevertheless, he presented it 'with befitting ceremony' on 7 October and later confirmed that it 'appeared satisfactory when installed in the Empress's Palace'. He suggested that some press coverage would please the Abyssinians, and the Foreign Office accordingly arranged for items in *The Times* and *The Illustrated London News*.[7]

The throne's proportions were taken from an eighteenth-century Chinese throne in the V&A associated with Chien Lung (fig.139). It was made of gilded teakwood, had a red velvet cushion and stood on a plain

[7] Times, *3 Dec 1925*; ILN, *19 Dec 1925.*

139. Imperial throne. Chinese, Qing dynasty, about 1775–80. Carved lacquer on wood. Used as a model for the final design for the Abyssinian throne. W.399–1922

A MEMENTO OF PRINCE RAS TAFFARI'S VISIT TO ENGLAND LAST YEAR: THE NEW THRONE PRESENTED BY THE BRITISH GOVERNMENT TO THE EMPRESS ZAUDITU.

PRESENTED BY THE BRITISH GOVERNMENT TO THE EMPRESS REGENT OF ABYSSINIA: A NEW THRONE.

teak base with five steps, which was carved with the Amharic inscription and had its details picked out in gold (fig.140). The Abyssinian crown of Menelik surmounted the back, and some of the decorative details were taken from the Cyprus throne, but it was still unmistakably a European design of the 1920s. Despite Bentinck's reservations, it apparently 'gave every satisfaction' to the recipients, and the donors also felt they had acquitted themselves honourably. In a letter to Cecil Harcourt Smith on

140a & b. Throne presented by the British Government to the Empress Regent of Abyssinia in 1925. Teak with gilding, designed and made by Laurence Turner. Illustrated in the *Illustrated London News*, 19 December 1925

141. Master's Chair of the Art Workers' Guild. Oak. Designed by William Richard Lethaby (1857–1931), probably for Kenton and Company, and made by G.B. Bellamy in 1893

27 January 1941 Eric Maclagan felt that 'looking at it after an interval of fifteen years it seems to me quite a creditable performance for us both to have been associated with'.

They had certainly faced some unusual problems, though of course any commission of this kind generates its own specific requirements. The question of whether the end product really rose to the challenge is almost irrelevant. The real importance of the Abyssinian throne lies not in the object itself, but in the light its story sheds on the rather prosaic realities underlying the creation of even the grandest ceremonial chairs. The throne was a presentation item, so the designer did not have to consult the wishes of its eventual user. Instead, and as so frequently happened, he found himself working for a committee. This had a limited budget, but was anxious to commission something which would be appropriate and usable as well as showy. Although the members were able to outline some of their requirements at the outset, these firmed up

142. Bardic chair made for the Cardiff Eisteddfod in 1938 by the Brynmawr Furniture Workshops. Archives of the Welsh Folk Museum

143. Bishop's throne at Coventry Cathedral (built 1956–62), designed by Basil Spence with sculpture by Elizabeth Frink

and developed as the design process took place and the final product bore little resemblance to their original ideas. Both the form of the throne and the details of its decoration were inspired by the past, but the end result still reflected the fashions of its day.

Twentieth-century problems

The story of the Abyssinian throne also serves to introduce some of the new problems which have beset the ceremonial chair in the twentieth century. Reading between the lines, it is easy to sense a certain embarrassment and lack of conviction about the whole project amongst the donors. A similar crisis of confidence seems to have affected the design of many twentieth-century ceremonial chairs. There are several reasons for this, of which the most fundamental is perhaps the changed nature of government and society. The bishop's *cathedra* or the royal throne suggests a system of government where authority flows downwards and outwards

144. Chair for the use of the Master at high table, Pembroke College, Cambridge, presented by F.C. and J.C. Pritchard in 1954. Designed and carved by David Pye and made and upholstered by R. Lenthall at the Royal College of Art. Black bean wood and bent plywood, with Bombay rosewood coat of arms and morocco upholstery

[8] But cf. David Carradine, 'The Context, Performance and Meaning of Ritual: The British Monarchy and the "Invention of Tradition", c. 1820–1977' in Hobsbawm and Ranger, *for details of one attempt to circumvent this problem which has been at least partially successful.*

[9] *Adolf Loos,* Samtliche Schriften, *Vienna, Verlag Herold, 1962, p. 27.*

from a single, divinely appointed ruler. If the government are the elected representatives of the people, the throne loses much of its meaning as a symbol of authority, and too great a display of pomp and circumstance comes to seem inappropriate.[8]

This also ties in with the distaste for ornament which has characterised much twentieth-century architecture and design. Our modern incomprehension of the language of symbol and ceremony can be seen as both a contributing factor to this distaste, and a result of it. The disappearance of decoration has usually, and to some extent justly, been associated with the early twentieth century and the birth of Modernism. In a celebrated article on *Ornament and Crime* published in 1907, for instance, the architect and designer Adolf Loos announced that 'cultural evolution is equivalent to the removal of ornament from articles in daily use' citing the urge to scribble on lavatory walls and the criminal classes' fondness for tattooing amongst his evidence.[9] Yet the roots of this distaste go back further. The Arts and Crafts movement of the nineteenth century, for instance, was by no means anti-ornament. Yet its emphasis on structural honesty and truth to materials was largely a reaction against the Victorians'

145. Design for Queen Alexandra's throne in the House of Lords. Holland and Sons, with annotations by Edward VII dated 1901. E.6–1985

lavish and frequently meaningless use of decoration. The very plain chair which Lethaby produced for the Art Workers' Guild in 1893 (fig.141) already suggests one of the paths open to the designer of the ceremonial chair in the following century.[10]

This trend towards greater simplicity inevitably robbed the ceremonial chair of much of its potential magnificence, but not necessarily of its dignity. It is interesting to contrast the bardic chair produced in 1938 by the Brynmawr Furniture Workshops (one of a group of industries set up by the Quakers in the depressed Clydach Valley in the early 1930s[11]) in fig.142 with its Victorian predecessor in fig.103. At Coventry, Basil Spence put the bishop's throne and the stalls for the clergy opposite those for the choir and placed clusters of stylised thorns above them. These rise above the throne into a canopy, which is crowned with a gilded copper mitre made by Elizabeth Frink (fig.143).[12] A Master's Chair designed by David Pye was presented to Pembroke College, Cambridge in 1954 (fig.144). One of the donors was the furniture manufacturer Jack Pritchard, the

[10] Ed. Sylvia Backymeyer and Theresa Gronberg, W.R. Lethaby 1857–1931: Architecture, Design and Education, London, Lund Humphries, 1984, p. 149.

[11] 'Helping those who help themselves', Country Life, vol. lxxviii no. 2028 (Nov. 30 1935), p. cxxiv.

[12] Basil Spence, Phoenix at Coventry, London, Geoffrey Bles, 1962, pp. 101, 104, 14, pl. 44.

146. Two chairs used for the first part of the coronation of George V and Mary in 1911. The design is taken from an armchair of about 1680 at Knole. Gilded walnut frames by Howard and Sons, with velvet upholstery woven by Warners. Royal Collection

[13] *Jack Pritchard,* View from a long chair, *London, Routledge and K. Paul, 1984, p. 156.*

[14] Architectural Review, *vol. 116, no. 694 (July 1954), pp. 50–1.*

founder of Isokon and perhaps best remembered for his work with Marcel Breuer in the 1930s. He had got to know David Pye through their work at the Furniture Development Council.[13] At the time the chair was described as 'uncompromisingly in the style of the mid-twentieth century',[14] a verdict which still holds good.

Modernist ceremonial chairs have however remained the exception rather than the rule. Many more designers have continued to recycle historic styles in the same way as their Victorian predecessors. Twentieth-century notions of architectural good manners have made straight reproductions seem the most appropriate solution in certain historic settings. It is understandable that when Edward VII commissioned a throne for Queen Alexandra's use in the House of Lords (fig.145), Holland and Sons designed one almost identical to Barry and Pugin's original for Queen Victoria (fig.69). Too great a respect for historical accuracy and good taste can however have rather unexciting, not to say unremarkable, results. For George V and Queen Mary's coronation in 1911 'it was very properly decided that both the Thrones and Chairs of State should be not only of English make throughout, but should be of characteristically English types'. Both sets were copied from the famous collection of

147. One of a pair of thrones made for the coronation of Edward VII and Alexandra in 1902. Made by Carlhian and Baumetz of Paris, under the supervision of Sir Joseph Duveen, art dealer and benefactor of the Tate and the National Gallery. Gilded wood with embroidered crimson velvet upholstery. Royal Collection

seventeenth-century royal furniture at Knole which was mentioned in chapter III. The chairs of state in fig.146 were taken from an upholstered armchair of about 1680. However, it proved necessary to gild the walnut frames at the last moment because they looked 'too sombre' when set up in the Abbey.[15]

Many more designers have continued to reinterpret historic forms and motifs to meet the demands of the present day, in a way which is already familiar from earlier chapters and the account of the Abyssinian throne. Two examples of this process are the lush throne produced for Edward VII's coronation in 1902 and rather misleadingly described at the time as 'Renaissance' (fig.147), and the more recent sanctuary chair shown in fig.148. Yet this method requires an extensive knowledge of historic styles in a period when few designers have received much training in this area. It has also been harder to find craftsmen used to producing elaborate carving and other traditional kinds of decoration, thanks to the decline in the popularity of ornament. Even if these difficulties are overcome, the subject

[15] *Coventry.*

148. Design for a chair and prie-dieu for Theydon Bois, Essex, dated 1956. By Laurence Edward King OBE, FSA, FRSA, FRIBA (1907–1981). E.606–1981

seems to have spurred few twentieth-century designers to the level of creativity shown in the chair in fig.149, which was designed by Sir Edwin Lutyens for the new headquarters he had just built for the BMA in Tavistock Square. This recalls historical examples such as fig.7, yet has a distinctive presence largely due to its quirky solidity.

More recently, the postmodernist movement has been associated with a revival of interest in historical styles and symbolic decoration. It might at first be thought that this could also herald a renaissance for the fortunes of the ceremonial chair. It is certainly interesting to compare a design like Charles Jencks's 'Spring Chair' (fig.150) with the Lutyens chair. The 'Spring Chair' is part of a symbolic scheme of decoration designed by the architect for his own London house, which is 'basically about the Cosmos with rooms decorated to suggest the five seasons (including the Indian Summer around the Sun Stair and the Moonwell)'.[16] The shell form of the chair is intended to suggest Spring, and a painted Wedgwood shell plate and small onyx pyramids symbolising the sun are incorporated in its decoration. Both these chairs are the work of architects; both designs refer to historical styles and include symbolic decoration; both have a monumental presence which has been achieved by enlarging their

[16] Charles Jencks: symbolic furniture, *exhibition held by Aram Design Ltd., London, November 1985.*

149. President's Chair of the British Medical Association, presented by the Australian branches in 1925. Black bean wood with red leather upholstery, designed by Sir Edwin Lutyens (1869–1944). W.42–1987

150. The Spring Chair. Designed by Charles Jencks, 1984. Medium-density fibreboard. W.13–1986

proportions as well as their size. Yet the 'Spring Chair' is not a throne, but rather a piece of domestic furniture which draws on the symbolic and ceremonial associations of the chair. These are kept firmly within quotation marks: the intention is clearly to delight and amuse, rather than inspire awe. Reviewing an exhibition of seating of this kind in New York in 1988, a professor of philosophy was led to comment that the 'postmodern period of the chair is the postmodern period of human power'.[17] In other words, because we no longer have confidence in ourselves and in authority, we can no longer take these associations seriously either. The crisis of conviction which has overwhelmed the ceremonial chair during the twentieth century has not been overcome. It has simply taken us in a new direction. The chair has ceased to be a serious emblem of authority, and become a plaything instead.

[17] *Danto, p. 14, p. 16.*

BIBLIOGRAPHY

This is not a comprehensive bibliography, but an overview of the major sources used for this book. It includes some material which is not discussed in the final text (usually for lack of proper documentation). It is arranged according to the same subject headings as the book itself: the first section in particular includes more general works which have been quoted more than once. Works listed in the bibliography are identified in the footnotes by the surname of the author, or by whatever abbreviation is given here. Sources of less general relevance are instead given in full at the proper location in the footnotes.

Introduction

Hollis S. Baker, *Furniture in the ancient world: origins and evolution 3100–475 B.C.*, London, Connoisseur, 1966

Victor Chinnery, *Oak furniture: the British tradition*, Woodbridge, Antique Collectors' Club, 1979

H.M. Colvin, *A Biographical dictionary of British architects 1600–1840*, London, John Murray, 1978

(*Dictionary*) Geoffrey Beard and Christopher Gilbert (eds.), *The Dictionary of English furniture makers*, Leeds, Furniture History Society/W.S.Maney & Son Ltd., 1986

(Eames 1971) Penelope Eames, 'Documentary evidence concerning the character and use of domestic furnishings in England in the fourteenth and fifteenth centuries', *Furniture History*, vol.vii (1971), pp.41–60

(Eames 1977) Penelope Eames, *Furniture in England, France and the Netherlands from the twelfth to the fifteenth century*, London, Furniture History Society, 1977 (published simultaneously as vol. xiii of *Furniture History*)

Furniture of Western Asia, a conference held at the Institute of Archaeology, London, 1993 (proceedings to be published)

(Heal) Heal Archive, National Archive of Art and Design (AAD.2–1978, SU24). Two box files of notes and cuttings, with the titlepage 'Chairs historically considered, illustrated with specimens of every variety as used for state ceremonial or domestic purposes by the most celebrated men and women of the age, past and present, collected and arranged by Ambrose Heal 1885–6', but including a number of later additions

(*HOKW*) H.M. Colvin (general ed.), *The History of the King's Works*, London, HMSO, vols.i–vi, 1963–73

Eric Hobsbawm and Terence Ranger (eds.), *The Invention of Tradition*, Cambridge, Cambridge University Press, 1983

Joan Liversidge, *Furniture in Roman Britain*, London, Tiranti, 1955

Percy Macquoid and Ralph Edwards, *The Dictionary of English furniture*, London, Country Life, 1954

Eric Mercer, *Furniture 700–1700*, London, Weidenfeld and Nicolson, 1969

Iorwerth C. Peate, 'Some Welsh light on the development of the chair', *Apollo*, vol.xxviii (Dec. 1938), p.299–300

Gisela Maria Richter, *The Furniture of the Greeks, Romans and Etruscans*, London, Phaidon, 1966

(*Rococo*) Exhibition catalogue, *Rococo: art and design in Hogarth's England*, Trefoil Books/Victoria & Albert Museum, 1984

Ivan G. Sparkes, 'Royal and civic furniture', in *Queen Elizabeth II: a Silver Jubilee memento of High Wycombe*, 1977

Clive Wainwright, *The Romantic interior*, New Haven and London, Yale University Press, 1989

Ole Wanscher, *Sella curulis: the folding stool: an ancient symbol of dignity*, Copenhagen, Rosenkilde and Bagger, 1980

(*Wren Society*) *The Volumes of the Wren Society*, Oxford, Oxford University Press for the Wren Society, 1924–43, vols.i–xx

Cathedrals and churches

G.W.O. Addleshaw and Frederick Etchells, *The architectural setting of Anglican worship*, London, Faber & Faber, 1948

Francis Bond, *Wood carvings in English churches*, London, Henry Frowde/Oxford University Press, 1910

J. Charles Cox and Alfred Harvey, *English church furniture*, London, Methuen & Co., 1908 (2nd ed.)

Alfred Heales, *The History and law of church seats or pews*, London, Butterworths, 1872

C.A. Ralegh Radford, 'The Bishop's throne in Norwich Cathedral' and 'The Synthronon in western usage', *Archaeological Journal*, vol.cxvi (1959), pp.114–32

Gerald Randall, *Church furnishing and decoration in England and Wales*, London, Batsford, 1980.

Fred Roe, *Ancient church chests and chairs in the home counties*, London, Batsford, 1929

Royal thrones and chairs of state

'The Thrones of the World', *Furniture and Decoration*, vol.v, no.2 (Feb.1 1894), pp.26–7

Hugh Murray Baillie, 'Etiquette and the planning of state apartments in baroque palaces', *Archaeologia*, vol.101 (1967), pp.169–99

Martin Drury 'Two Georgian chairs of state and a state canopy at Knole', *Furniture History*, vol.xxi (1985), pp.243–50

Philip Grimes, 'Support of kings' [furniture at Grimsthorpe], *World of Interiors*, Dec 1987, pp.96–8

Gervase Jackson-Stops, 'The sixth Earl of Dorset's furniture at Knole', *Country Life*, vol. clxi, nos. 4170&1 (2 & 9 June 1977), p.1495–7 & 1622

Simon Jervis, '"Shadows, not substantial things". Furniture in the Commonwealth Inventories' in *The late King's goods* (ed. Arthur Macgregor), London and Oxford, Alistair McAlpine/Oxford University Press, 1989

(Juxon chair) Ralph Edwards, 'The "Charles I" chair', *Country Life*, vol.lxiii, no.1621 (11 February 1928), pp.176–7, Charles R. Beard '"King Charles I's" chair: a new theory', *Connoisseur*, vol.lxxx, no.320 (April 1928), pp.228–31, Charles E. Russell 'The Juxon chair and the Bower portraits of King Charles I', *Old Furniture*, vol.iv (1928), pp.98–9 and letter on p.242, and letters to the editor from Edwards and Beard in *Connoisseur*, vol.lxxxi, no.324 (August 1928), p.264

Sir Guy Francis Laking, *The Furniture of Windsor Castle*, London, Bradbury Agnew & Co., 1905

Westby Percival-Prescott, *The Coronation chair*, London, Ministry of Works, 1957

Hugh Roberts, 'Royal thrones, 1760–1840', *Furniture History*, vol.xxv (1989), pp.61–77

H. Clifford Smith, *Buckingham Palace*, London, Country Life, 1931

R.W. Symonds, 'The Royal X chair: its development from the XVth to XVIth centuries', *Apollo*, vol.xxv, no.149 (May 1937), pp.263–8

Laurence E. Tanner, *The History of the coronation*, London, Pitkin, 1952

Peter Thornton, 'Canopies, couches and chairs of state', *Apollo*, vol.c (October 1974), pp.292–9

Alexandra Wedgwood, 'The throne in the House of Lords and its setting', *Architectural History*, vol.xxvii (1984), pp.59–68.

Official bodies and societies

Rosamond Allwood, 'Wood carving: the "high art" of Victorian furniture making', *Antique Collecting*, vol xxiii, no. 10 (March 1988), p.49–54

(Graham 1988) Clare Graham, 'A Masonic Master's Chair made by John Connop in 1814', *Furniture History Society Newsletter*, no. 92 (November 1988)

John Hardy, *India Office furniture*, London, British Library, 1982

John Harris, 'William Chambers and the Society's President's Chair', *Journal of the Royal Society of Arts*, vol.cxiv, no.5117, (April 1966), pp.429–32

T.R. Hewitt, 'Some unrecorded masonic ceremonial chairs of the Georgian period', *Transactions of the Quatuor Coronati Lodge*, 1965, pp.135–9 [a continuation of E.T. Joy's article]

E.T. Joy, 'Some unrecorded masonic ceremonial chairs of the Georgian period', *Connoisseur*, vol.clix (1965), p.160

David Learmont, 'The Trinity Hall Chairs, Aberdeen', *Furniture History*, vol.xiv (1978), pp.1–8

(*Livery Companies: V&A*) *An exhibition of works of art belonging to the livery companies of the City of London*, Victoria and Albert Museum, London, 1927

(*Livery Companies: Country Life*) 'The furniture of the livery companies of London', *Country Life*, vol.lx, no.1553 (23 October 1926), pp.635–8

Commemorative chairs

'Our industries: the Bucks chair trade', *Furniture and Decoration*, vol.iii, no.3, March 1 1892, pp.41–7

Geoffrey de Bellaigue, 'The Waterloo Elm', *Furniture History*, vol.xiv, 1978, pp.14–18

(*Catalogue*) *Official Descriptive and Illustrated Catalogue of the Great Exhibition, by authority of the Royal Commission*, London, 1851

(*Foudroyant*) *Nelson's Flagship the 'Foudroyant'*, trade catalogue produced by Goodall Lamb and Heighway, Manchester, 1904

(Graham 1990) Clare Graham, 'Seats of Learning', *Country Life*, vol. clxxxiv, no. 35 (30 August 1990), pp.108–9

F.G. Kitton, 'Some famous chairs', *The Strand Magazine*, 1 Oct 1893

W.A. Thorpe, 'An historic chair', *Country Life Annual*, 1952

G.W. Yapp, *Art Industry: Furniture Upholstery and House Decoration*, London, Virtue & Co., c.1876

Zdzislaw Zygulski, Jr., 'Shakespeare's chair and the Romantic Journey of Isabel Czartoryska', *Apollo*, vol. lxxxii, no. 45 (Nov.1965), p.392–7

The twentieth century

L.B. Coventry, 'English coronation chairs', *Connoisseur*, vol. xcix (June 1937), pp.280–3

Arthur C. Danto, 'The seat of the soul' in *397 Chairs*, New York, Harry N. Abrams Incorporated, 1988 (based on an exhibition at the Architectural League of New York)

E.H. Pinto 'Coronation chairs and royal thrones', *Apollo*, vol. lvii (June 1953)

INDEX